Brian Heeney, an Anglican priest, completed the D.Phil. degree at Oxford University. In 1971 he was appointed Master of Champlain College at Trent University in Peterborough, Ontario, Canada.

STUDIES IN BRITISH HISTORY AND CULTURE

VOLUME V

A Different Kind Of Gentleman

A Different Kind of Gentleman

*Parish Clergy as Professional Men
in Early and Mid-Victorian England*

BY
BRIAN HEENEY

Published for
The Conference on British Studies and Wittenberg University
by ARCHON BOOKS

Library of Congress Cataloging in Publication Data

Heeney, William Brian Danford, 1933-
    A different kind of gentleman.

    (Studies in British history and culture; v.5)
    Bibliography: p.
    Includes index.
    1. Clergy—England. I. Title. II. Series.
BR759.H4   253′.0942   76-17329
ISBN 0-208-01460-8

© Brian Heeney 1976

First published 1976 as an Archon Book,
an imprint of The Shoe String Press, Inc.,
Hamden, Connecticut
for
The Conference on British Studies
and
Wittenberg University
Springfield, Ohio

Printed in the United States of America

To Charles Feilding
with respect, affection, and gratitude

CONTENTS

Illustrations

(following page 34)

FOREWORD

Studies in British History and Culture was founded in January, 1965, as a joint publishing venture of the Conference on British Studies and the University of Bridgeport; Stephen Graubard and Leland Miles were the Senior Editors, and the New York University Press was printer. Three volumes were published in the series under this arrangement, the last being in 1970. A five year hiatus then occurred when the University of Bridgeport decided that it could no longer fund the series. Fortunately, Wittenberg University volunteered to become co-publisher with the conference and with Archon Books. Since that time the series has published one book.

The intention of the conference and the editors in establishing the monograph series was to publish works of vigorous research, original interpretation, and literary grace which fell between the regular article and the full length book. The editors were especially seeking works which would challenge traditional viewpoints or advance new theses and works which would integrate particular events with larger themes.

In the fifth volume in the series—*A Different Kind of Gentleman*—Brian Heeney challenges the view of many social and church historians as to the role and status of the clergy by arguing that there was a developing professional ideology among early and mid-Victorian clergymen. He derives this "ideal" clergyman from the works on pastoral theology written by a "relatively small group of experienced clergymen," and observes that the advice given in these manuals "was strikingly unaffected by the peculiarities" of ecclesiastical party controversy. This latter point is a view suggested by Horton Davies in his *Worship and Theology in England*, vol. III, but it is given added significance by this close study of the writings of the pastoral theologians. The work also contributes to the growing literature on the emergence of the professions in Victorian England.

Stephen Baxter
Leland Miles
Senior Editors

Acknowledgements

I am indebted to the C. D. Howe Memorial Foundation and to the American Council of Learned Societies for generous fellowships which enabled me to make two research trips to Britain. Both the University of Alberta and Trent University granted me sabbatical leaves, and the president and fellows of St. John's College, Oxford, kindly allowed me to occupy a room in that college and to enjoy the hospitality of their senior common room. Outstanding among the many individuals who have given me valuable assistance are Charles Feilding, A. J. Russell, Michael Hurst, Brian Harrison, John Walsh, and the late Dr. G. Kitson Clark. I am grateful for the help of the librarians and staff of the Bodleian Library, Pusey House, St. Paul's Cathedral Library, the British Library, and Church House in Liverpool. Deryck Schreuder kindly read parts of early versions of these chapters and gave me encouragement when it was needed, and Marian O'Brien efficiently typed various versions of the text. Albert Hayden, editor of the series in which this book is published, has been most helpful. All of my children cheerfully accompanied me twice across the Atlantic and, through it all, my wife Goodith has provided the support and love which made it possible.

Parts of Chapter II appeared earlier in the *Journal of Religious History* and *The Historical Magazine of the Protestant Episcopal Church.* I am grateful to the editors of those journals for permission to use this material. Permission to reproduce illustrations has been granted as follows: from the Curators of the Bodleian Library, Oxford, for those of J. W. Burgon, R. W. Evans, and W. W. Champneys; from the Governors of Pusey House for those of Robert Gregory, Henry Mackenzie, Ashton Oxenden, and Samuel Wilberforce; from the Leeds City Libraries for that of Edward Monro. The photograph of Harry Jones was taken from a portrait which hangs in the parish rooms of the Church of St. Vedast in the City of London; I am grateful to Mr. N. P. Mander for drawing my attention to this portrait.

I am indebted to James Retallack for his assistance in proofreading and in making the index.

B. H.

TRENT UNIVERSITY
Peterborough, Canada

xii

I

A VIEW FROM THE INSIDE

THE PURPOSE of this book is to sketch a picture of the ideal English parish clergyman in the first part of Victoria's reign. The viewpoint is that of a relatively small group of experienced clergymen who wrote works of pastoral theology for the guidance of their younger colleagues. They belonged to different schools of churchmanship and represented different theological traditions. Individually, they had various experiences of urban, suburban, and rural parishes, and they attached different degrees of importance to various aspects of clerical character and parochial work. One thing they shared was a deep interest in improving the quality of pastoral care in the Church of England.

In most cases this concern for parish ministry dominated all their other ecclesiastical interests, whether the relations of church and state, the tension between revealed truth and scientific knowledge, the theory of the sacraments, foreign missions, or fine points of theology, liturgy, or ceremonial practice. This was true of Charles Bridges, R. W. Evans, John Sandford, Edward Monro, Ashton Oxenden, and both J. J. and J. H. Blunt; it was so in the cases of Henry Mackenzie, W. W. Champneys, and Harry Jones, as well as most of the other figures whose names appear less frequently on these pages. (For biographical notes, see Appendix I.) Certainly Samuel Wilberforce made important contributions in other spheres, and he is commonly remembered for his reform of the episcopal office and for his debate with Thomas Huxley rather than for his advice to ordinands. J. W. Burgon had strong (usually reactionary) views on many matters outside the practice of the parish ministry. But neither in his case, nor in that of Wilberforce, did other matters intrude much into their works on pastoral care.

The picture of the Victorian clergyman's life and work presented on these pages is a view not only from inside the church, but also from the perspective of one particular group of clergymen. Obviously there were many angles from which churchmen viewed the parish clergy, and from which very different pictures would be taken. The standpoints of the bishop, of the archdeacon, even of the rural dean, were those of authorities in the ecclesiastical structure; although they often shared the concerns and interests of pastoral theologians (in several cases bishops and other authorities themselves wrote handbooks) their connection with the parish clergy who were subject to their power was not simply that of a professional adviser. Parishioners of different ranks and classes adopted attitudes to the clergy which were peculiar to their stations in life, which reflected traditional class political and social grievances and feelings, as well as local concerns that had little in common with the dominant interests of the pastoral writers. The gentry of many Victorian rural parishes expected the parson to be a friend, perhaps a companion in sport as well as in society. Patron-squires naturally looked for clerical neighbors who would fulfill these expectations, and whose families would be welcome guests in their own houses. On the other hand the poor of the parish looked to the incumbent for charity, and the tradesmen for patronage.

Outside the congregations of the established church opinion about the clergy was often hostile and sometimes shrill. Jeremy Bentham considered them defenders of abuses and skilled practitioners of "political fallacies."[1] Although not all Nonconformist Christians were actively unfriendly (the Wesleyan attitude to the church was characterized by a prominent Methodist in 1868 as "independence without enmity")[2] militant Dissenters lumped the clergy together with the aristocracy as the enemies of political and religious liberty. In Edward Miall's opinion those of the clergy who were not themselves "supernumary members of lordly houses" were lackeys of lords, dependent on the ruling landed class for their appointments, preferment, and social life, and therefore wholly committed to the maintenance of the political and social status quo. Clergymen, Miall believed, were well-equipped for this role,

> wielding, to appearance, the dreadful sanctions of religion—almoners, usually, of parochial funds and the great man's bounty—conduits through which may flow to bowing tradesmen the custom of the rich—having access to every house, able to assume an air of authority, and, in virtue of their office to work upon religious fears and affections. Fifteen thousand clergy [are] thus dependent on the one hand, and powerful on the other—to the aristocracy pledged servants, to their flocks supreme dictators—stationed at convenient intervals over the length and breadth of the land, and thus coming into contact with society at all points.[3]

A different political interpretation of the clergyman's pastoral work was that of working-class radicals. Early in the nineteenth century the clergy had been among the chief villains of radical leaders. Condemned as tithe owners and oppressors of the rural poor, they were also seen as agents of the governing classes appointed to keep poor men ignorant, or at least to restrict their knowledge to diverting and innocuous matters of religion. Chartist leaders damned the clergy as

> a sable society of gentlemen wearing broad hats and deep garments; who possess a great part of the wealth and power of the world, and would have all, as a reward for keeping mankind in decent ignorance and bondage.[4]

Just as they were the object of rural laborers' anger in the Swing riots of 1830, so in the 1870s the clergy again suffered unpopularity among the leaders of the militant agricultural workers, and were again accused of using their pastoral office, particularly their influence in village schools, to impede social reform.[5]

It is not impossible to recognize the parson so hated by militant Nonconformists and radicals in the works of the pastoral theologians. They wrote a good deal (often in immoderate language) about how to cope with Dissent, and many of them were certain that the maintenance of political stability was an important pastoral function. However, their motives in recommending conservative attitudes, institutions, and activities were frequently more benign than those imputed to them by militant Nonconformists and radicals. More important, they did not believe that the clergyman's calling was mainly political or social (conservative, radical, or whatever). Rather it was understood as the religious calling of a religious man, and, although they recognized many desirable secular aspects of the pastoral vocation, the handbook writers insisted that these were peripheral and not central.

No image of the Victorian clergyman, whether that of Trollope's "parson of the parish,"[6] that of Edward Miall, or that of the Chartists, is likely to be an accurate reflection of any particular parish priest. No more is the ideal image of any of the pastoral theologians likely to be a precise representation of reality. How far any particular parish clergyman conformed to any contemporary conception of what a parson was or should be is a matter that can only be determined by carefully examining individual clerical careers. To test the validity of such preconceptions in particular regions, counties, dioceses, or towns requires extensive and detailed research of the sort pioneered by Diana McClatchey in her *Oxfordshire Clergy, 1777-1869* (Oxford, 1960). No full examination of local records lies behind this study. But it may be useful to those who engage in such research to have before them the ideal parson of the pastoral theologians, a group of Victorians who loved their subject and understood him rather better and more sympathetically than most.

There is another value in this enterprise. The handbooks and other materials upon which this book is based constitute a distinctively professional literature. They reveal developments in the clerical profession analogous to changes in both the legal and medical professions which are of considerable interest to sociologists as well as to social historians.

In his book *The Sociology of the Professions* (London, 1972) Philip Elliott distinguishes between "status professionalism" and "occupational professionalism," and he uses this distinction as the basis for an interpretation of nineteenth-century changes in law, medicine, and the church.[7] In preindustrial England of the eighteenth century the term "professional" denoted a person of high social status, closely associated with the governing landowning class, able to live a leisured and cultured life, equipped with a good (but entirely general) education, and responsible for what Elliott calls a "problem area" in society. The professional man, whether a physician, a barrister, or a clergyman, was not expected to have expert knowledge or skill, nor to accommodate himself to a professional style of life; nor was he thought of *primarily* as a person who dispensed specific services for fees or salary. In that society those who had particular skills and performed specific functions and who worked primarily for monetary reward were not necessarily considered professional men.

As society became industrialized in the nineteenth century occupations became increasingly specialized and this concept of professionalism changed. Occupations which in the old society were denied professional title acquired that name, but on new terms. The right to be described as professional depended less on social status and much more on skill, on expert educational qualifications tested by examination. In the old professions of law and medicine the actual work done by the professional man, and the evidence that he had the necessary knowledge to do it, were of increasing importance. Conversely his social status was less emphasized; attorneys and apothecaries, formerly subprofessional branches of law and medicine, gained professional standing. Underlying this change in emphasis from "status professionalism" to "occupational professionalism" in the medical sphere was the increasing importance and volume of scientific knowledge considered necessary for the medical practitioner. In the case of the lawyer changes in landownership and the expansion of modern agriculture, commerce, and industry brought a volume of complicated procedures which demanded much precise legal knowledge and expertise.

In the nineteenth century clergymen were being subjected to pressures similar to those which affected their contemporaries in law and medicine. The Evangelical revival and the Oxford Movement in their different ways encouraged the clergyman to acquire more theological knowledge, more technical, pastoral, and homiletical skills, and a more distinctively clerical style of life than had been customary in the eighteenth-century church. The respect for utility that lay behind much reform in church and state just before and during Victoria's first years on the throne put further pressure on the clergy to define their role in a society that felt increasingly uncertain about rewarding any but its useful members. So did popular anticlericalism. Strong emphasis on the virtues of work and duty (expressed, for example, in the works of Samuel Smiles) had much the same effect. To these pressures was added another which predates the eighteenth century, but which was much strengthened by the occupational specialization that accompanied industrialization: the gradual withdrawal of occupations from under the umbrella of the old nonspecialist clerical profession. The legal and medical professions and the central public service had all been emancipated from the church long before the industrial revolution. But in the later eighteenth century there remained an enormous array of non-religious functions performed by the clergy: educational, medical, judicial, and administrative. During the nineteenth century most of these were detached from the clerical profession either by new or reformed secular professions or by the agencies of an expanding state. As this occured clergymen were driven to consider and to define their necessary functions, the occupations which justified their status, in the new sense their profession.

Evidence of this effort at redefinition is clear in the Victorian literature of pastoral care. In the handbooks of the pastoral theologians, in discussions at clerical meetings, church congresses, and meetings of convocation, and in the columns of the church press there are many indications of a new professionalism among the parish clergy of the Church of England. Gone, by 1870, was general acceptance of the old "status professionalism." No longer was it considered acceptable for a clergyman to be simply a classicist and a gentleman, friend of the squire, almoner to the poor, and patron of local tradesmen, who had few but the vaguest notions of any distinctively clerical role beyond the obvious liturgical and preaching functions. Victorian pastoral writers minutely described areas of particular professional responsibility. They discussed techniques to be learned and skills to be acquired which they believed would assist the clergy to discharge their responsibilities. (See chapters III and IV.) Far from satisfied with general gentlemanly education as a preparation for parish ministry, most handbook writers pressed for some form of additional theological and pastoral training, a deliberately professional edu-

6

cation for a professional ministry. A good many were not only prepared to accept nongraduates into the ministry (they were being ordained anyway) but looked for ways of training men deliberately recruited from social classes well below the level of gentility. Pastoral writers encouraged the association of parish clergymen in clubs and larger professional bodies. They often wrote about the need for continued theological reading after ordination. Some at least urged modification of the traditional patronage structure to make way for a system of appointment and promotion based on professional merit. (See chapter V.) These writers also set before their clerical readers an ideal priestly *persona*, that of an unworldly gentleman whose moral qualities placed him apart from the society to which he ministered. This professional character was at least as important an element in the make-up of the model clergyman as were adequate theological knowledge and pastoral skills. (See chapter II.)

The works of the Victorian pastoral theologians show that, in many respects, the parochial clergy were becoming a profession in the modern sense during the first three-quarters of the nineteenth century. The process, however, was far from complete. Anthony Russell, a sociologist, has noted three ways in which the clergy failed to conform to the new professional standards by the early 1870s: they had not gained control of the institutional church (parliament, patrons, and bishops still largely possessed this); frequently they were subject not only to criticism but also to correction by laymen concerning the way they performed their professional duties; they lacked a national "reward structure and career pattern" based on professional merit.[8] In other respects as well the process of conversion from a status to an occupational profession was incomplete. Although distinct clerical character was established as an important professional qualification, many pastoral theologians also insisted that the clergy should possess many of the qualities and certainly the education of lay gentlemen. Social status was still very important in gaining preferment and promotion, and it remained so despite the infusion of a good many nongentlemen into the ministry in the mid-Victorian period. Furthermore, although different types of pastoral and theological training were advocated, and although many ordinands received such training, professional education never became a requirement for ordination. Finally, although the pastoral theologians did manage to define the professional religious functions of parish priests, the clergy themselves stubbornly refused to confine themselves to those roles. Indeed none of the pastoral theologians thought they should do so. Some clergy exercised the art of management and developed a considerable capacity to direct a parochial staff and organize complicated parish machinery; they harnessed the science of administration to the sacred ministry itself. The Victorian clergyman was expected to be a generalist, to perform services which required trained intelligence and general knowledge rather than specific skills, to fill the gaps in local public service not yet occupied either by other professional men or by government bureaucrats. The secular occupations of parish ministers, although they usually constituted a different mix than that common among the pre-Victorian clergy, were quite as numerous as they had been in the eighteenth century. Thus while the works of Victorian pastoral writers demonstrate a narrowing of strictly professional concern, the same evidence shows an extraordinary breadth of clerical involvement, including many apparently secular activities which were not always undertaken from secular motives.

The pastoral theologians were the heralds and theorists of a revival of pastoral care in the early Victorian Church of England. Like all new style parsons of their time, especially those influenced by the Evangelical or Oxford movements, they felt little but contempt for the pastors of the preceding age. Victorian clergy enthusiastically developed a myth of eighteenth-century ecclesiastical corruption and worldliness, of pastoral apathy and incompetence. As they looked around for reasons why workingmen ignored the church and why Dissent flourished, they found the explanation largely in the church's neglect of the people in the century or so before 1830.[9] They complained about political bishops, about pluralism and nonresidence, and about gross inequities in eighteenth-century clerical incomes. But they reserved their most vigorous condemnation for the alleged secularity, laziness, and inefficiency of the parish clergy. Identified in society with the squirearchy, the clergy "gambled and rode, drank and swore" and frequented "theatres, horse-races, balls and taverns."[10] Lacking any form of regular theological or pastoral training, most Georgian clergy were accused of being incompetent as well as lax and worldly. Their sermons (when they were original, neither borrowed nor bought) were said to have been "of unreadable dulness . . . dry, cold, and uninviting." Prayers as well as sermons were dreary, church buildings were uncared-for, "furniture, vestments, and accessories of worship were sordid and slovenly."[11]

These conditions were thought to have extended well into the nineteenth century when they were gradually corrected by Evangelical fervor or Tractarian devotion, or both.[12] Against the grievous neglect and corruption of the recent past, the developing spiritual life and the quickened pastoral activity of the second and third quarters of the nineteenth century seemed to provide a sharp contrast. Churchmen in the middle years of the century had feelings comparable to those of a patient miraculously cured of a mortal sickness, grateful for the deliverance and determined to avoid contagion again. "Our own generation has witnessed recovery from the dismal apathy which had so long prevailed," wrote the editor of the *Quarterly Review* (himself a parish clergyman) in 1857:

> True theology has revived, pluralities have been abolished, residence enforced, services multiplied, schools built; while the clergy as a body have displayed a zeal, a diligence and a liberality which will bear comparison with the brightest periods of ecclesiastical history.[13]

Twentieth-century historians have greatly modified the Victorian picture of the eighteenth-century church, and the contrast between religious practice in 1800 and that in 1850 now seems less sharp than it appeared to the pastoral handbook writers of the mid-nineteenth century. Norman Sykes showed that there was careful conscientious pastoral and episcopal work in the eighteenth century: the sick were visited; many faithful communicants attended the Eucharist (although it was not as frequently celebrated as in the Victorian period); many bishops confirmed and ordained as diligently as contemporary conditions permitted.[14] Although there was no general movement to provide special training for ordinands, some eighteenth-century bishops and others attempted to improve the generally low standard of pastoral and theological training.[15] Things were not as "bad" in the eighteenth century as the Victorians thought, even by Victorian criteria. Nowadays the standards of judgement themselves have changed. The laicized parson of the eighteenth century is more attractive to many twentieth-century churchmen than is the sanctified model constructed a hundred years ago. The spirituality of Georgian times seems less arid to us than to our forefathers in the last century.[16] Furthermore we may question their belief in a simple connection between religious revival (Evangelical or Anglo-Catholic) and pastoral renewal. It seems more than likely now that anxiety about anticlericalism and the rapid growth of Dissent, parliamentary legislation, widespread pressure for practical reforms in administration, and developing professional standards were of considerable importance in bringing about change in the pastoral ministry. We may doubt too, as did Dr. Kitson Clark, whether the change from Georgian apathy to Victorian fervor was as rapid or as complete as the Victorians would have us believe.[17]

When all these qualifications are made, however, there remains no doubt that there was a renewal of parish life in the early and mid-Victorian church, and that the central figures in that renewal were the parish clergy.[18]

II

CLERICAL CHARACTER

To EARLY Victorian pastoral theologians what a clergyman was mattered quite as much as what he did. He was set apart from the local community to be an example as well as a pastor. Ashton Oxenden, the Evangelical rector of Pluckley, put it as well as any:

> He is not merely to go through a certain routine of duties; he is not to put on a little official sanctity now and then. He is to be a living pattern to Christians, a living rebuke to sinners.... He is, in short, a man of consecrated character.[1]

Evangelicals were particularly inclined to stress "consecrated character" as the chief mark of a true pastor and to dismiss the change of status effected by ordination as of secondary importance. In Charles Bridges's view neither apostolical succession nor proper conformity to ecclesiastical procedures and laws compensated in any way for lack of personal sanctity and living doctrine in the clergyman.[2] By the 1860s even those who took a high view of episcopal ordination or who obviously valued the secular position of the established church were clear that "consecrated character" was the most important attribute of a clergyman. Samuel Wilberforce made this point to his ordinands in 1860, and in the following year the broad churchman John Sandford observed in his Bampton Lectures that "prescriptive and traditionary claims of every kind are comparatively lightly regarded, and the deference once accorded to station must be in great measure earned by personal qualities."[3]

By his distinct character and sacred style of life the clergyman was marked off from his lay contemporaries. The apartness of a clergyman in society was much emphasized by Tractarian and Evangelical pastoral theologians. In 1850 Edward Monro said that "the life of the clergyman should be a standing protest against the life around him." He should feel profoundly alienated from society, so much so that for him to live in the world at all would be painful. Evangelicals took the same view. The clergy, said Charles Bridges, were "in a peculiar sense men of God," and a writer in the *Christian Observer* described them as "God's peculiar property."[4] Such writers maintained both a theory of clerical apartheid and a doctrine of ministerial moral superiority. "The everyday life of a Christian pastor," wrote Oxenden, "instead of being as the life of men in general, should be sacred." By sacred he meant "unworldly . . . heavenly-minded . . . separate from sin." "To be a pastor of souls," said Henry Manning in 1846, "is to be under a vow which binds us to the highest devotion we can attain. . . . Relaxed habits—blameless in our lay brethren—are not innocent in us."[5]

Very few "relaxed habits" were beyond reproach in Victorian clergymen. Relaxation itself was suspect and often equated with indolence. Even morally innocent amusements such as botany, geology, and gardening might encroach on the pastor's clerical labors.[6] Although pastoral theologians expressed no doubts about the enjoyment of hunting and shooting by Christian laymen, these sports were widely condemned as unclerical.[7] So were card playing, theater going and dancing, even by the relatively easygoing broad churchman Harry Jones whose *Priest and Parish* stood out among the handbooks for its common sense. "A walzing priest," he wrote, "probably offends all except those lax and indifferent people whom a little offense might improve. We have no order of dancing dervishes in the English church." The high church author of *Clerical Recreations* was more vivid:

The young lady will scarcely care to recognize as her proper spiritual guide and friend her partner at last week's ball; and the dancing priest may well find it difficult to assume at once his ministerial character towards those with whom he has shared . . . small-talk and trifling nothings.[8]

Cricket, archery, and billiards all attracted the disfavor of the defenders of clerical character. It was all too easy for the country clergyman to become addicted to the company of his landed neighbors and to lose his "taste for seriousness and piety" in a continual round of dinner parties. Of course some social visiting was expected of the clergyman, but when he did dine with his neighbors the ideal clergyman should never completely relax:

> He will never forget what and where he is. . . . Even the stranger will discover his office, not by his black clothes, nor yet by unseasonable intrusion of subjects too solemn for the occasion; but by that indescribable propriety, that modest dignity, that gentleness and serenity which is derived from the habitual exercise of his profession.[9]

Rather than attempt an index of prohibited amusements and entertainments, Ashton Oxenden simply denounced all those "of a frivolous or boisterous nature . . . anything which brings him [the clergyman] into contact with ungodly persons" and "anything . . . likely to disturb and overbalance his religious tone." As a parting shot he warned his clerical reader to avoid all public places of recreation where "ungodly persons" were apt to congregate. Frivolity threatened that highly desirable clerical quality of "gravity," that "sobriety and solidity" which was identified as a key factor in correct clerical presence.[10]

It is a relief to find all these restrictions on clerical recreation damned as "sour puritanism" by one contemporary who felt, in 1863, that they stopped good men from offering themselves for ordination. Not only did they unduly restrict the clergyman's personal freedom; they also kept him from fulfilling his ministry among ordinary folk. Just because he was forbidden to join them in their avocations, to mix with them in their leisure activities, the priest was prevented from really knowing them as human beings. This, in turn, made it difficult for him to preach effectively or to advise them on moral matters. The same critic also protested

13

against the developing insistence on distinctively clerical dress and appearance:

> If [the clergyman] so far yields to the dictates of nature and commonsense as to pitch his razors into the fire, and wear a beard, he is looked upon as a suspicious character, and perhaps has a bishop down upon him. The same if he puts a comfortable covering on his head.[11]

He seemed to think this strictness a Protestant aberration. In fact it was much more general and certainly represented the views of many high church and Anglo-Catholic writers like Cecil Wray, whose ideal curate always wore distinct clerical dress, or Henry Lloyd who insisted that "our behaviour, our dress, our places of resort, our occupations, should always plainly be those of God's clergy."[12]

Some clergymen in the 1850s and 1860s evidently found the shield of clerical clothing and abstention from lay amusements inadequate protection against the corruption of secular society. On 6 February 1850 "a country rector" wrote to the *Guardian* seeking support for the establishment of "an exclusively 'clergy club' in some central situation" in London. Such a club would be a comfortable but simple *pied à terre* for parsons from the country. Equipped with a drawing room, library, and dining rooms, it would substitute a chapel where prayer would be read by some member of the club every morning and night, for the usual billiard rooms and smoking rooms. Shocked by episcopal patronage of the established "flash clubs" he observed that the "mixture of members in all existing clubs" and their "luxuries, expenses and worldliness" unfitted them for clergy patronage. In fact such a clergy club was formed at 13 Henrietta Street eight years before this letter appeared in the *Guardian*, although it may not have survived until midcentury. The "original members" of this club included 219 clergy, among them the Tractarian pastoral theologian Edward Monro and the prominent broad churchman Henry Alford; but no English bishops at all appear on the list. In the late sixties an organization known as the "Clergy Club and Hotel Company" seems to have operated a London club and hotel chiefly, but not exclusively, for the clergy.[13]

Important external support for the "consecrated character" of a clergyman and the style of life which flowed from it was provided by the law and the tradition that ordination, unlike the admission rite to any other profession, had a binding effect; the ordained minister was permanently committed to his sacred duty. It was "a great help to us in our ministerial course," wrote Henry Lloyd, to know that "'once a priest always a priest' is true in this world and in the world to come."[14]

Church law was precise about the permanent effect of ordination. According to canon seventy-six "no man being admitted a Deacon, or Minister, shall from thenceforth voluntarily relinquish the same, nor afterward use himself in the course of his life as a layman, upon pain of excommunication." Furthermore, relatively recent statute law had exempted clergymen from jury duty, and barred them from sitting in parliament or engaging in trade. Although the clergy were given limited legal permission to farm their glebes, and there was a tradition of clergy undertaking illegal outside work of other kinds, activities of these sorts could not reverse the effect of ordination. Neither voluntary renunciation of orders nor excommunication could restore to a clergyman the rights of a layman.[15]

For most clergy the indelibility of their orders was at least as much a matter of theology as of law. Anglo-Catholics, high churchmen, and Evangelicals all agreed on the impossibility of abandoning the clerical character once it had been assumed formally. Ashton Oxenden warned the prospective deacon that he was on the brink of an irreversible change:

> You are now like a sailor standing at the water's edge, and surveying that vast ocean on which your lot is soon to be cast. . . . Now, therefore, count well the cost. Hesitate ere you launch irrevocably on the eventful voyage. . . . Once set apart for the work of the ministry, there is no receding from it.

Strikingly similar was Samuel Wilberforce's view that the words of vocational commitment "cannot be unsaid," that the deacon's "vows cannot be read backward." Indelibility of orders was a doctrine much emphasized by Anglo-Catholics like R. M. Benson, founder of the Society of St. John the Evangelist, and Edward Monro.[16]

Most pastoral writers thought that a priest was not only indelibly marked by his ordination, but also committed by that rite to a full-time and life-long ministry. "He must be a man wholly given to his work," wrote Joseph Baylee, the Evangelical founder of St. Aidan's College in Birkenhead, "or he must be content to be looked upon in society as a careless shepherd of the Lord's Flock." This total commitment had no parallel in other professions. As James Pycroft put it, "a man may be half a doctor, or half a lawyer, but he cannot be half a minister of Christ." There must be "no earthly parentheses in our ministerial life," Samuel Wilberforce told his ordinands, "always we are the messengers of Christ; . . . all our life and every part of it is embraced in the wide-spreading engagements of the Christian Ministry."[17]

Such views, together with the legal prohibition against trading clergy, undoubtedly fortified the clergyman's sense of superiority and separation from ordinary men and ordinary occupations. They also inhibited efforts to develop patterns of ministry which would be both economically self-supporting and more closely connected to the secular ways of the middle and lower classes. During the 1850s Archdeacon W. H. Hale made proposals for an "extended diaconate" which would provide for a temporary and part-time ministry. The idea was taken up in convocation, but a committee of that body reported in 1859 that legal difficulties prevented a self-supporting ordained ministry in the Church of England. Furthermore the indelibility of the diaconate excluded "those who could give the service of a *time*, but not the service of a *life* to this especial . . . work." Consequently the committee went on to propose a form of subdiaconate (really a lay order) with "duties . . . so adjusted that it may include persons of all ranks and classes of society." Some of these subdeacons were to receive stipends, whereas others were to serve without payment. All would be perfectly free to resign at any time without any problem of indelibility.[18] Such ministers would not be ordained clergymen, and the proposal (which led to an order of lay readers) did nothing to introduce nonprofessional or short-term clergy into the ministry of the Church of England. Legal, theological, and customary inhibitions prevented any such step. In the minds of most Victorian pastoral writers the clergyman's profession was permanent as well as full-time. The distinct character of a clergyman, held to be essential for professional effectiveness, would be compromised by the knowledge that it could be abandoned.

This was the common view, but it was not universal. Outside the ranks of the clergy alarm was expressed about the growth of "a priestly feeling" which, by the middle sixties, was thought to infect clergymen of all parties, and not just those in the high church tradition.[19] Among ordained writers Harry Jones, author of *Priest and Parish* and a broad churchman, was remarkable for his suspicion of the doctrine of distinct clerical character and for his dislike of the contemporary understanding of indelibility. He thought that true clerical sanctity "is seen in a yearning sympathetic regard for his fellow rather than in an air of separation," and he was upset about the fate of those disillusioned clergy who felt totally unfit for their posts but who could not escape the indelibility of their orders. Such a man, wrote Jones, must choose between hypocrisy and starvation:

> A bewildered disappointed priest, confessedly, obviously unfit for his holy craft, may ply it without restraint, even if he preaches that which he doubts; but is liable to penalties directly he gives it up to undertake some business which he can discharge without dishonesty.

For the sake of honesty and humanity the law must be changed and the restrictive theology of indelibility cast aside.

Harry Jones's views on idelibility were extraordinary. Less exceptional, but still unusual, was his opinion that an ordained minister in good standing might engage in secular work not directly connected with pastoral or educational duties. Pointing to the example of St. Paul, Jones joined with others (men who on the general matter of distinct clerical character were with the majority) in stressing the desirability of a nonprofessional ministry in which ordained clergymen might earn their living in secular work. As we have seen such a ministry never developed.[20]

Distinctiveness and moral and spiritual superiority were not the only features of clerical character. Pastoral theologians spent much effort considering particular personal qualities of the ideal pastor, and also the failings to which he was especially susceptible. The lists of virtues were lengthy. Nearly all included a simple interest in people and the capacity to accept and work easily and happily with all sorts and conditions of men. Few expressed this better than William Cadman, a well-known Evangelical, who observed that a pastor must be "prepared to deal with men as they are" and must never "stand aloof from the repulsive, the vicious, the alienated." He must attract and encourage fellow laborers among his faithful parishioners, realizing that he alone cannot do all the work that must be done.[21] Such "love of souls" was the source of sympathy, a quality understood as the capacity to appreciate and to feel the tenor of his parishioners' lives. Insistence on this quality is virtually universal among the handbooks, manuals, and other professional literature. Sometimes the emphasis is unusual. John Sandford, no man to discount the value of order and stability in the social structure, wrote that sympathy

> merges all distinctions in the thought that they [the parishioners] and the priest are fellow-sinners and fellow-sufferers equally beholden to the same grace, thrown together for a while in the journey of life, and to be forever associated at its close.

Unlike the members of other professions, a priest could never treat people impersonally. Whereas "the medical man goes his professional round, and can inflict suffering, or pronounce death on his patients without much, if any, disturbance to his own feelings," wrote the author of one handbook, the pastor "who traverses the same trying path must sympathise with all those upon whom he is called to attend."[22]

Sympathy sometimes seemed to mean an almost total immersion in the lives of the pastor's flock. No one felt this more strongly than the Tractarian incumbent of Harrow Weald, Edward Monro, whose own activity among railway navvies, seasonal agricultural workers, and others was remarkable for its sympathetic understanding. The practice of pastoral sympathy as Monro defined it made enormous demands upon the time and the imagination of the pastor, and required a quality he called "elasticity," which to others was simply "patience."[23]

The ideal parson of the Victorian pastoral theologians was a hard worker, industrious, punctual, systematic, and thorough. Numerous schemes were produced to inculcate these virtues in the young clergyman. No doubt this emphasis was characteristic of the mid-Victorian professional ethic generally, but the independence of parish incumbents, and their remarkable freedom from external constraint was thought to exaggerate the temptation to idleness and procrastination. James Pycroft, author of *Twenty Years in the Church*, complained that endowments often gave parsons an unhealthy sense of security unrelated to their professional performance. He cautioned his fellow clergy that

> public opinion checks you less than other men. . . . The surgeon, the lawyer, the tradesman, are all wound up to concert-pitch; the patients, the clients, or the customers serve as masters to keep them to their work. Hungry competitors are ever waiting to pounce upon their errors and take their places.

In contrast, the clergyman must provide his own discipline; he must

> daily calculate his progress, and study economy of time, punctuality, and business-like habits. He must reflect that he is beset by an insidious temptation, being more his own master than any other man; and must take care lest the blessing of independence should prove in eternity his ruin.[24]

Fears that clergy were neither systematic nor industrious in their pastoral work were stimulated by a fierce leading article in the *Times* of 10 September 1856. It accused the clergy of being "the idlest among us," and went on to insist that the ecclesiastical authorities

> require of them the actual performance of their duties, make them render a daily account, have an efficient and permanent superintendence, and . . . a system of promotion according to service and merit.

Although it was answered at length on 6 January 1857 in a letter from Abraham Hume, an incredibly active Liverpool incumbent, the *Times'* attack on clerical character remained in the memories of handbook authors for many years.

Whereas idleness was a special temptation for country clergymen, many writers considered frantic activism a peculiar danger to conscientious town parsons. There was a real hazard that such a man would conform unconsciously to what one speaker described as

> the beau-ideal of a modern clergyman . . . a versatile combination of an athlete, a showman, a popular lecturer, a sanitary commissioner, an accountant, a relieving officer, a savings' bank manager, a district visitor, a general adviser on every conceivable topic from the choice of a trade or profession to the best method of cultivating plants in window pots in a blind alley.[25]

Distracted in mind and exhausted physically, the activist urban priest often failed to reserve the time necessary for prayer, study, and reflection, "the essential requisites of the ministerial character."[26] In other words he could become secularized even though his worldliness was ecclesiastical in focus and perhaps philanthropic in aim. "Time was," wrote James Pycroft,

> when balls and hunts and amusements of all kinds were the best of baits; but now the hook must be better covered, . . . a platform-meeting, a deputation to entertain, speeches to get up, . . . an agricultural school . . . the church to renovate . . . clerico-political meetings, the clergy meeting periodically in chapters, agitating church questions and the rights of the Church.[27]

A variety of other dangers and temptations surrounded the Victorian clergyman, ranging from the ambition exhibited by priests who were "perpetually enquiring into the value of benefices" to over-indulgence in domestic pleasures. Hypocrisy ("outside professional religion" Samuel Wilberforce called it) was to be avoided at all costs. It was an insidious danger especially threatening to a self-conscious priesthood. Walter Hook wrote that "hyprocrisy . . . lies under the question which is so often asked, is this or that clerical."[28]

The clergy did not escape temptations to unchastity about which all respectable Victorians were so sensitive. Edward Monro, an advocate of sacramental confession, thought that danger arose from the privacy necessary to confidential interviews between a priest and individual female parishioners. Oxenden warned that clergymen should be very cautious in visiting females without a third person present. The author of *Hints to Young Clergymen* went beyond advocating caution; he attempted to instill fear, observing that

> habitual mixing of the sexes . . . tends to rob a man of all vigour and energy of mind, and quite unfits him for speaking with anything like authority or the weight of personal influence from the pulpit.[29]

The early and mid-Victorian pastoral theologians' emphasis on distinct clerical character did not produce a sudden or uniform revision of clerical personality in the Church of England. For one thing, there were contradictions among the elements of the ideal, contradictions which were not easily resolved. Strict aloofness from wordly preoccupation was to be combined with remarkable sympathy for human beings; perpetual industry was to be united with scholarly and spiritual repose. Furthermore, the pastoral theologians were not the only people who laid claim to the parsons of England. Neither were the pastor's co-professionals nor his bishop the only people whose expectations mattered to him. His patron and his parishioners (of various social grades) expected qualities in him, as they anticipated activities from him, which often conflicted with each other and also with the professional writers' ideals. Trollope's parson who "is not averse to some occasional truces" with the devil, who "dislikes zeal," and is repelled by the "over-pious young curate" must have seemed more attractive to many country squires than the professional paragons constructed in the manuals of Oxenden and Monro and the ordination addresses of Wilberforce and Mackenzie.[30]

In any case there was still much clerical behavior quite at odds with these ideals. In 1854 W. J. Conybeare commented amusingly on five types of "clerical adventurer," all of whom he found present among his contemporaries. Of these, perhaps the most characteristic was the "safe man," whose whole object was to promote his career by providing evidence of "soundness" without ever giving offense. Prudence was his watchword, and "in all his actions he is distinguished by a sense of the plausible and becoming." Having risen to the episcopate by being always safe, he was remembered after his death as a man "serenely soothing and tranquilising to the church." He did no serious harm to the church, but he omitted to do much good either.[31] Evidently respectable worthlessness and worldliness had not completely triumphed over colorful corruption. In 1860 the upper house of Canterbury Convocation was shocked to receive a petition from the mayor of Derby and a number of influential laymen, protesting against "offences against religion and morality committed by persons in holy orders," and Bishop Tait deplored the "melancholy fact" that

> at this time, when by God's mercy the Church is exerting herself more than in past years, and there is more zeal among clergymen and more regard for the peoples' souls . . . strange and unheard-of scandals have certainly accumulated more than at any former period.[32]

Against safe men, as against scandalous clergy, the pastoral writers fought by constructing a lofty professional ideal. When they imagined the ideal parson, they usually used the traditional pictures of shepherd and father. The last chapter of J. W. Burgon's *Treatise on the Pastoral Office*, for example, is a meditation on the clergyman as shepherd ("this, after all, is the sum of ministerial duty"), and Charles Bridges considered "the true portrait of a Christian pastor" to be "that of a parent walking among his children." Rather more up-to-date was Henry Mackenzie's military image of the clergy as "officers" in the "Kingdom of the Redeemer."[33] One implication of this imagery is clear. However kind, sympathetic, compassionate, and thoughtful they might be, shepherds, fathers, and officers were all easily distinguishable from sheep, children, and ordinary soldiers. So should the clergy of the established church be distinct from their people.

Along with their demand for a professionally self-conscious clergy, most early and mid-Victorian pastoral commentators continued to insist that those who were indelibly set apart for the ministry of the established church should share the tastes, manners, and learning of lay gentlemen. J. H. Blunt, a high churchman well-known for his handbook *Directorium Pastorale*, was typical in his assertion that "whatever spiritual gifts may be theirs by holy living and ordination . . . the clergy are required to be men whose character and attainments are such as to place them in the foremost ranks of the educated classes." "If there are those among the clergy who do not come up to this ideal of the Church of England," he went on, "the fault lies in the administration of her rulers, not in her constitution."[34] University graduation was generally thought to guarantee gentility, and those who most frequently asserted the need for this quality were the staunchest defenders of university education for ordinands and opponents of "side doors, not to say back doors into the service of the sanctuary."[35] Some writers simply assumed that clergymen were gentlemen without bothering to argue the point. J. W. Burgon, for example, describing the problems and difficulties of pastoral visiting, observed that "those of the highest grade we visit on equal terms: conventionally their equals on the social scale; as a matter of fact, their equals (to say the least) in education."[36]

The Victorians inherited this ideal of the gentleman-pastor from the recent past. In the Restoration period, and at the beginning of the eighteenth century, the social status of the English clergy was far more humble, and recruits to the profession were often sons of shopkeepers and farmers, and sometimes the children of laborers.[37] The incomes of eighteenth-century curates were pitifully low, and the value of most livings quite inadequate to support a gentle style of life. This had changed by the last half of the eighteenth century with the effects of the agricultural revolution and the enclosure movement. As glebe and tithe owner, the parson, along with the squire, was normally a promoter and beneficiary of local enclosure acts. Frequently he commuted a modest tithe into a valuable extension of his property, thus enhancing his position as a landowner.[38] The clergy were also active in promoting new and profitable methods of agricultural practice, and as new land was brought under cultivation in the parish they extended their tithe rights. The result of all this was a great increase in landed wealth under the control of the clergy, and consequently a rise in their social position. A profession formerly despised for its poverty now became an acceptable vocation for the squire's younger son. Thus there developed the tradition that country parsons must be gentlemen, preferably married gentlemen, resident in comfortable and commodious parsonages. The inhabitants of these dwellings, according to J. A. Froude, were "continually in contact with the people, but associating on equal terms with the squires and the aristocracy." Froude wrote that in

1830 "the average English incumbent" farmed his own glebe, kept horses, "shot and hunted moderately and mixed in general society."[39]

Froude's picture of the pre-Victorian clergy, like the gentleman-ideal itself, was not an accurate reflection of reality either before or after Victoria's accession. Many country clergymen, whatever their pretensions to gentility, could not afford to keep up socially with their landed neighbors. Others had few pretensions. W. J. Conybeare's famous article on "The Church of England in the Mountains" revealed the existence, in 1853, of about one thousand "peasant clergy" who held livings in Wales and northern England, and who (according to Conybeare) came from farm homes marked by ignorance, coarseness, intemperance, and immorality. One Westmoreland gentleman, who thought his local incumbent "by no means a bad specimen," remarked that

> no servant is kept in his house, and several of his sons have been brought up to handicraft trades. We are very good friends, but he could not visit my house. . . . His sister was waiting-maid to a friend of ours.[40]

Curates were, and remained, poor, insecure, and sometimes uncouth.[41] Furthermore, as more and more churches were built to accommodate the urban masses, an increasing number of pastoral charges were in districts without resident gentry, without the support of tithes and glebes, surrounded by an alienated poor and a frequently hostile middle class. In these situations gentlemen-parsons were often ineffective. Certainly they were not attracted to such cures and the social origins of urban clergy were, in fact, commonly lower than those of country clergy. This was a fact recognized by the general public and remarked by Anthony Trollope who noted that, whereas the "country parson is all but the squire's equal . . . the town incumbent . . . in the estimation of many of his fellow-townsmen is hardly superior to the town beadle."[42]

In these circumstances some of the early and mid-Victorian clergymen who took a special interest in their profession attacked the ideal of clerical gentility. Many felt that a church whose clergy were tied to the social and political élite could never hope to gain the loyalty of the whole people, much less be a reconciling agency among the segments of a divided society. In 1833 Thomas Arnold described the ideal Christian ministry as a "beautiful chain to link the highest and the lowest together through the bond of their sacred office." It followed that "the ministry should contain persons taken from all [classes]."[43] Much the same opinion was repeated by churchmen of various sorts in various ways during the next three decades. Henry Mackenzie, a pastor with both urban and rural experience, developed a theory that the three orders of ministry were divinely designed to minister to the three elements of society. Unfortunately the Church of England had undermined the divine plan by limiting its ordained ministry to gentlemen. Mackenzie believed that effective ministry was possible only if pastor and people were of the same social class. By excluding both the lower middle and working classes, the church, he thought, had "lost myriads who might otherwise have been gathered to her fold."[44]

The "gentleman-heresy" (as Hurrell Froude had called the gentleman-theory of ministry) could induce a form of snobbery particularly effective in alienating the middle class. "That the church has lost its hold on trade is too generally acknowledged to require illustration," remarked the *Guardian* on 10 December 1856, "and among the causes of that alienation it is impossible not to place the social and political position of the clergy." J. H. Blunt felt that the socially superior clergy ministered easily to the rural poor, but he cautioned that it was sometimes difficult for a pastor to allow himself to be entertained by tradesmen. Professionally he must visit their homes on their terms, yet he found it very hard to persuade his wife that tradesmen and their ilk were suitable people with whom to dine.[45] To some critics an obvious means to gain the goodwill of the middle class for the church was to relax the social demands made of ordinands. "Perhaps the middle classes would be a little more attached to the church," wrote one correspondent in the *Guardian* on 7 December 1864, "if they . . . could say of the clergyman sometimes, 'He is one of us.'"

According to some writers élite clergy were rendered professionally incapable by their social status. This was said to be especially true of those working among the urban poor. On 30 January 1867 the *Guardian* reported a six-hour meeting between a number of workingmen and a group of Christian ministers and laymen, including several prominent Christian Socialists. The social distance between clergy and workers (and the educational distance which was part of it) was repeatedly alleged as a reason why the working class showed such little interest in the church. A cabinetmaker, for example, reported that "working-men felt that clergymen had separated themselves from the rest of the world, and that religion was no longer a thing they could identify with their daily life"; and a carpenter complained that "the clergy thought themselves superior to the working man, and if the latter did not bow down to him, he was a marked man."

This alienation was felt by sensitive slum priests who often found themselves lonely although earnestly engaged in energetic social work and surrounded by masses of people. Robert Gregory, the vigorous incumbent of St. Mary's, Lambeth, attributed this sense to a lack of corporate feeling among slum dwellers, whom he thought merely an "aggregation of independent isolated atoms." But Abraham Hume of Liverpool knew that Gregory was wrong. There was, he found, a distinctive group culture among the poor:

> The little community [of the poor parish] takes a tone which all are expected to adopt, and the social requirements, the customs of the place, become more rigid than the laws of the Medes and the Persians.

The clergyman's sense of isolation had its origin, not in an absence of slum community consciousness, but in the parson's own incapacity to recognize that culture. Because of his elevated social status and his alien pattern of life and education he had no part in the life-style of the slum community.[46] As a result he was often lonely. Hume spoke of the "frequent want of sympathy which chills and unnerves" such priests, and Gregory vividly pictured the gentleman-pastor's feeling of aloneness in his ministry:

> His voice is not repeated by echoes. . . . He is ever surrounded by non-conductors of sound. . . . Think of what it would be like to talk separately to 100 people, to attract them to accept or believe something to which they were indifferent or opposed . . . and you may form some notion of the insurmountable labour which is assigned to the incumbent of an overgrown metropolitan parish.[47]

26

"Highly educated gentlemen" were not fitted to communicate with the poor. "Do what they will in the way of visitation," said Henry Mackenzie, "they cannot *live* among them." Mackenzie wanted a rougher sort of pastor to mix among the poor in urban parishes. John Burnet, the vicar of Bradford, sought curates of a humble social grade, and he recommended the ordination of worker-deacons who could, without embarrassment, visit the homes of their fellow workers from seven to nine o'clock in the evening. Unless he were extraordinarily tough minded, a gentleman-ordinand would naturally prefer country and village life to isolation, overwork, and poverty in the slums. But even in the country, warned Charles Bridges, he would miss conversation "with men on his own level—men of good breeding, education and intelligence"; conversely, his university background might make it difficult to communicate with his rustic flock.[48]

The most obvious objection to the gentleman-ideal of ministry in the fifties and sixties was the quantitative one. At a time when hundreds of incumbents were needed for newly consecrated churches, and when higher standards of pastoral care created an unprecedented demand for assistant curates, clergy were in alarmingly short supply. Although in the forties the number of clergy had kept pace generally with population growth, this was not true in the fifties, and even less so in the sixties.[49] Ordinations to the diaconate numbered 622 in 1850 and 632 in 1853; but they declined generally through the later fifties and reached a low of 489 in 1862. A gradual rise took place thereafter, and the 1850 figure was surpassed in 1874, although in the following year the number again dropped to only 614.[50] The low figures for 1860, 1861, and 1862 caused alarm, especially as those ordinations occurred at a time when much attention was being directed to the shortage of clergy in many urban districts. Although the *average* number of parishioners to each clergyman remained constant at just over one thousand,[51] this average masked huge variations. Not only were many country cures very small; some inner city churches, especially those in the City of London, had become depopulated. In Liverpool, on the other hand, the ratio was one priest to four thousand people, and in metropolitan London the average was one clergyman to every forty-eight hundred parishioners, although this too concealed great variations. Archdeacon Charles Thorp reported that in Newcastle there was only one clergyman to every seven thousand souls, and the situation seems to have been worse at Bradford.[52] In the late fifties and early sixties, professional opinion was nearly universal that a proper ratio would be one clergyman to two thousand parishioners. To achieve this ideal situation in urban districts a hugely increased number of ordinands was required.[53] Yet it was becoming obvious by the early sixties that fewer educated gentlemen, graduates of Oxford or Cambridge, were offering themselves for the ministry than in former times. Thomas Markby, writing in the *Contemporary Review*, noted a substantial decline in the number of graduates who chose the clerical profession at a time when the number of those who matriculated at the ancient universities was rising. "While from Oxford and Cambridge fewer present themselves," wrote T. E. Espin in 1863, " . . . the non-graduates [literates] are greatly on the ascendancy." The number of literates ordained during 1862 was, in fact, three times greater than in 1841.[54]

Explanations for the decline of gentlemen-ordinands were several. The poverty of all but a few livings, and the poor career prospects of most clergy under the contemporary system of patronage were thought to discourage many.[55] Gentlemen expected substantial incomes, sufficient to maintain the style of life appropriate to their class and adequate to justify the considerable investment represented by a degree at one of the ancient universities. Witnesses before a parliamentary committee in the mid-fifties considered an income of between £300 and £500 adequate to maintain the traditional standard of living of an incumbent, and the church commissioners agreed with them. Most contemporary commentators felt £150 a satisfactory stipend for a curate, although some thought that £100 was an acceptable minimum.[56] Modest as these figures seem, they were wildly utopian in the church of the 1850s and 1860s. In 1854 Conybeare discovered only 1,174 livings worth over £500, and more than 8,000 worth less than £300. On Conybeare's evidence two-thirds of the parochial incumbents received less than the desirable minimum. Furthermore the average salary of the nearly five thousand curates was less than £100 a year.[57] According to W. G. Jervis, a man whose cause in life was relieving clerical destitution, the situation was no better in 1861, when he calculated that there were ten thousand clergymen in England, Wales, and Ireland who were paid less than £100.[58] Jervis frequently appealed in the letter columns of the *Guardian* on behalf of penurious and destitute clergy, of whom he claimed to know several hundred. On 21 December 1859, for example, he wrote of a man, six of whose children had

> been attacked with scarlet fever, and they have wanted clothes, firing, and every other requisite. . . . Their house is destitute of every comfort—no cooking vessels, only two beds and a crib; no change of sheets; a few chairs and a table complete their furniture.

A church containing such miserable poverty could hardly hope to attract sufficient recruits from the universities to fulfill its ministry. By comparison many of the new opportunities open to graduates, especially in government service, held better prospects.[59]

A few writers suggested that intellectual unsettlement generated by doctrinal disputes in the early sixties caused some to abandon the thought of ordination. One commentator, C. P. Reichel, cited the lack of challenge in preparation for the profession as a hindrance to recruitment at the universities:

> Clerical training has not kept pace with the training for other professions. And though at first sight this might seem rather to hold out an inducement to enter the ministry, as requiring less study and self-denial than other professions do, it may possibly act in the directly opposite way. There is a generous enthusiasm in youth which is not satisfied with that which costs no trouble.[60]

Alarm about the inadequate supply of university recruits, whatever its cause, moved some to question the customary social restriction on the pastoral profession. "Is it not extravagant," asked the *Guardian* on 10 December 1856, "to hamper ourselves with the idea of supplying all England with adequate spiritual ministrations through none but 'resident gentlemen'?" In any case the tradition was already being undermined. Noting that one-third of the ordinands in 1863 were nongraduate literates, T. E. Espin thought that half of the seven or eight hundred new deacons needed annually must come from nonuniversity sources. Rather than attempt to realize the impossible dream of a numerically adequate exclusive ministry he urged that prompt attention be given to the training of these socially inferior recruits.[61]

The alleged ineffectiveness of gentlemen as pastors to the middle classes and the urban poor, and the need to overcome a shortage of ordinands were two important reasons put forward for widening the social base of the church's parish ministry, for modifying or disposing altogether of the gentleman-theory of ministry. There were other arguments as well. The *Christian Remembrancer* assaulted the " 'gentleman-theory' of the priesthood" as "neither catholic nor apostolic . . . but simply and purely English." Theologically unjustified, it fed the pernicious social ambitions of the middle classes. Ordination candidates too often were "aspirants to gentility"; once ordained such men were peculiarly status conscious. In fact, unless an ordinand was born a gentleman, and so educated, the *Christian Remembrancer* thought he should "keep close to his character as a Christian priest in a quiet unobtrusive way." That character, not the status of a gentleman, was his proper ambition.[62]

Attacks on the ideal of gentility forced its defenders to do more than affirm its value. They were required to defend their affirmations, and they contrived to do this on several grounds. None was more common than the opinion that gentlemanly education and gentlemanly tastes assured a desirable unity between the clergy and the leaders of secular society: a unity essential to the well-being of both church and state. "I think it is a great blessing to us all," said Archdeacon C. A. Harris of Wiltshire,

> that our clergy and laity are brought up together upon one universal system and one platform up to the age of twenty-two. . . . We need go no further than Roman Catholic Ireland to see that there is nothing more inexpedient than that the clergy should from fifteen or sixteen become a caste. Their ideas are narrowed; they have associations and tastes which diverge more and more widely from those of the laity, and there springs up at that early period of life an antagonism which is never got over.[63]

Others shared this view. Indeed the prominent broad churchman Henry Alford judged this close educational association between clergy and laity worth the sacrifice of whatever superior theological or pastoral accomplishments separate clerical training might produce.[64]

Undoubtedly one of the virtues of this unity between the leaders of church and state was cooperation in maintaining the political and social status quo. On 10 December 1856, the *Guardian* observed that

> it is no small security for the peace of the nation that 17,000 men scattered throughout the country, in positions which give them access to the poor at all times when they are most open to influence, are connected in habits and prospects, by blood and acquaintance and prepossessions, with what has been called the upper 10,000.

In 1864 J. H. Blunt considered that the parish clergy formed "the only link" between the life of local parishes and the leaders of society, and that their influence was "most beneficial on the side of order and morality."[65] Without the security of a gentlemanly standard, feared the *Guardian* on 9 September 1863, "the clergy would be ranged, as they have been already in France, on the side of democracy."

Especially important to liberal churchmen was the church's pastoral relationship to the intellectual élite. To assure the respect of the intellectual community, no amount of clerical zeal and piety could replace a gentlemanly style of learning: "a highly cultivated clergy is required to lead the religious thought of a highly cultivated people."[66] According to Harry Jones, a pastor must be a liberally educated gentleman, on a social and educational level with other professional gentlemen, if he were to remain influential in modern society. Should the clergyman abandon this position, and content himself with mechanical service as a religious functionary, people would "use him as the servant of the public and as a representative of respectability, but look elsewhere for the leaders of their thought." Nor was it only highly cultivated parishioners who benefited from a liberally educated clergy. Henry Mackenzie told ordinands in 1863 that a clergyman's position "as a man of education, refinement, and intelligence" qualified him to be the agent of informal parish education, a role of considerable importance especially in rural areas.[67]

Some frankly justified maintaining the tradition on financial grounds. Far from increasing the cost of ministry, restricting the profession to the upper classes actually cheapened it. In 1854 Conybeare suggested that the private income of the clergy at least equalled their professional income, so that "the clergy, while poor as a profession, are rich as a class." Archdeacon Sinclair pointed out a few years later that this private clerical wealth effectively doubled the amount of church endowment. Harry Jones thought that clerical fortunes had another virtue. He was certain they provided their possessors with a healthy independence which was basic to the "moral courage and purity" of many English clergymen.[68]

Contradicting those who saw university graduation and ordination as a means by which inferior persons climbed socially, James Pycroft viewed the tradition of graduate clergy as protection against middle class "ne'er-do-wells and adventurers." Once the ideal of gentility was compromised, remarked a speaker at the 1869 church congress, even if merely by the introduction of a few deacons or subdeacons into parishes where gentlemen dislike to minister, such persons

> after a few years passed on the moors or the hillside . . . may vanish and re-appear in the educated quarter of a wealthy town. . . . Men may ask to be sent to a village in Pisidia or Galatia, hoping to make it a stepping-stone to Athens or Corinth.

The only way to prevent this was to confirm the distinction between clergyman and layman, between ordained minister and lay reader. Such creatures as permanent deacons or subdeacons would only blur the distinction and create confusion. They would be no more pastoral help, and far harder to control, than scripture readers and other lay helpers.[69]

The Victorian clergy as a whole were remarkable for their devotion, energy, and vocational commitment. Among them were individuals of pastoral genius like Walter Hook of Leeds and William Champneys of Whitechapel, as well as men of courage and social sensitivity like George Bull, the ten-hours parson, and Edward Girdlestone, the agricultural laborers' friend. Yet despite such notable individuals, and despite the generally high level of clerical energy, pastoral effectiveness was seriously restricted in the mid-Victorian Church of England. It was limited by accelerating working-class detachment from the church. It was hampered by rigid parochial and diocesan structures inappropriate for ministry among mobile, increasingly urban, populations. It was inhibited too by divisions of churchmanship, by bitter strife between churchmen and Dissenters, and, at least among the intelligentsia, by the inadequacy of clerical scholarship to deal with the challenge of the higher criticism.

To these must be added the limitations of the professional and social ideals which were important elements in Victorian clerical self-consciousness. The professional ideal of a life distinct from the ways of ordinary men hardly encouraged that close sympathy with the common lot thought by all to be essential for effective pastoral care. The assertion of clerical moral superiority led to a double standard of behavior which could easily result in clerical hypocrisy and lay laxity. The contemporary conception of the indelibility of clerical character, and the common feeling that it could never be forsaken even temporarily, prevented the development of part-time or short-term ordained ministries. No doubt the continued social ideal of clerical gentility compromised this professional ideal of separation by drawing the clergy into intimate association with the lay élite. On the other hand, identification with the politically and socially powerful classes evidently hampered communication between pastors and the common people of their flocks. When a shortage of manpower forced the ordination of subgentlemen and nongraduates, such recruits were thought to be inferior, second-class clergymen. Rather than minister at their own social level, ambitious ordinands of this sort naturally aspired to the qualities of gentility which they knew would help them rise in their profession.

Although the ideals of separation and gentility are evident in the professional literature of all church parties, and were adopted by most of those who wrote about the profession, differences in churchmanship did result in different emphases. High churchmen, Tractarians,[70] and Evangelicals generally insisted on the professional ideal of detachment; but Harry Jones, the most systematic broad church pastoral theologian, was much less certain of its value and very sensitive to its dangers. On the other hand, although most pastoral writers disliked the prospect of a dominantly middle or working-class clergy, broad churchmen were especially insistent on the virtues of a liberally educated clergy. Some high churchmen, especially Tractarians with their strong theology of priesthood, actively promoted the ordination of humbler men if only to curb what they considered to be the irregular pastoral ministrations of lay helpers. Evangelicals, who cared comparatively little for ordination as such, but who shared the enthusiasm for expanding pastoral care, preferred to develop lay orders of ministry, socially inferior to gentlemen clergy and (in a general way) subject to their authority.

Not only did the professional and social ideals individually limit the effectiveness of pastoral ministry, they also conflicted with each other, and so created vocational tensions for conscientious clergymen. Could a gentleman of the world ever be a professional pastor on the new model? Would the two characters of pastor and gentleman not always be in conflict? The contradiction suggested by these questions lurked behind many a discussion of clerical character. Rarely was it made explicit, for few were prepared to sacrifice either ideal for the sake of consistency.

Top left: Robert Wilson Evans (1789-1866). *Top right:* Samuel Wilberforce (1803-73). *Bottom:* William Weldon Champneys (1807-75).

Top left: Henry Mackenzie (1808-78). *Top right:* Ashton Oxenden (1808-92). *Bottom left:* John William Burgon (1813-88). *Bottom right:* Robert Gregory (1819-1911).

Top: Edward Monro (1815-66). *Bottom:* Harry Jones (1823-1900).

III

THE RELIGIOUS CENTER

WRITERS who stressed the distinct and holy quality of clerical character also insisted on the centrality of religion in the pastor's work. His principal vocation was to cultivate the awareness and knowledge of God among his people and to encourage their obedience to the divine will. Certain professional activities were the accepted means of achieving these ends: leading in public prayer and worship; preaching the Gospel; celebrating the sacraments; consoling the sick; visiting the homes of the people; advising and admonishing individuals. Some primarily religious duties certainly affected secular relationships among members and sections of the pastor's flock. Parish visiting and parochial schooling, for example, had purposes which were secular, although these are not always easily separated from religious motives. Despite such ambiguities, and despite an important dimension of distinctly secular clerical duties, handbook writers had no doubt whatever that the pastor was called to an essentially religious work.[1]

No part of the parson's sacred duty was clearer, both in the ordinal and in custom, than regular and correct provision of divine service. Many Victorian pastoral writers offered advice for improving liturgical technique on Sunday mornings. Priests were urged to learn how to read clearly, and to give care to correct pronunciation and expression. Harry Jones suggested that clergymen with speech defects should seek expert therapy, and several writers advised the clergy to rely less on their books, to "address the exhortation, pray the prayers, declare the Belief, and preach the sermon."[2] Some sensitive and active early Victorian clergy found the effective performance of Sunday duty difficult when the forms of worship within consecrated buildings were rigidly prescribed by law and custom. Until the 1870s no variations whatever were permitted in the offices of the Prayer Book,[3] and it was usual to unite the service of morning prayer with the Litany and the Holy Communion at the main service on Sunday. Some churchmen in the 1850s and 1860s had a good deal to say about the inappropriateness of such worship for the poor, especially the urban poor. On Christmas Eve in 1851, for example, the *Guardian* complained about what it called "the usurpation of power and position by the middle class in this country in church matters." Because people of that class were offended by noise and "dislike show," therefore active congregational participation was discouraged and ornament banned from the churches. The *Guardian* thought that the "quiet, sober, orderly, and protected worship" customary in the Church of England seemed just dreary to the mass of the people. Bishops, alas, generally accepted this state of things, and the poor, whom the *Guardian* thought would be attracted by "appeals to the feelings," by "something more energetic and vigorous," simply stayed away.[4]

In fact clergy had been conducting special services for the poor over a great many years. Before Victoria came to the throne Walter Hook had held services for fishermen and seamen in a sail loft, and Augustus Hare had preached to rural laborers in barns.[5] The cottage lecture, which came to form an important tactic in the strategy of parish evangelism, was early recommended and described in H. C. Ridley's 1829 handbook *Parochial Duties*:

> The clergyman rings the bell . . . and on entering the room a short prayer is offered up. The portion of scripture is then begun in continuance with the last reading. From ten to thirty verses are gone through, almost word for word, with the distinct meaning of every passage and its reference to others, and explained as simply as possible. The whole passage is

then repeated in a sort of paraphrase, and lastly, the practical duties arising from its consideration are summed up under three particular heads. This, with the Lord's Prayer and another . . . occupies one hour.[6]

The effectiveness of such informal services was attested by many clergy in the 1850s and 1860s, and various other sorts of special evangelistic services were proposed and tried with the object of increasing the popularity of public worship. William Cadman, for example, had regular Monday evening services attended by nine hundred workingmen in his parish, and he wrote of special worship for coachmen and stable keepers in the west end of London. Parish mission services multiplied in London and elsewhere; Lord Shaftesbury successfully promoted informal "irregular" worship in theaters on Sundays; and both houses of Canterbury Convocation recommended that cathedrals be used for popular services.[7] One way to give reality and immediacy to worship was to connect it directly to local events. J. Erskine Clarke, for example, held a service in his Derby parish on the occasion of an execution; a great many attended, and Clarke wrote that he used the occasion to speak "plainly and strongly of the things which it becomes them to know."[8]

Of all the informal forms of worship and popular styles of address developed to attract the poor, none had wider appeal to mid-century Evangelical clergy than the open air meeting. In December 1856 the *Christian Observer* noted approvingly that "there are few of the large towns in which some or many of the clergy are not making this attempt to win the souls of careless sinners for Christ." Street services were instituted to attract those who, although they may have attended Sunday schools, had become "self-banished wanderers from the House of God."[9] Such services (which usually consisted of hymns, extemporaneous prayer, collects, and a sermon) evidently failed to draw masses of the working class to the regular ministrations of the church. Yet they were both widespread and popular in the 1850s. We read of "densely crowded" streets around W. Curling in Southwark as he preached "near the house in which a woman had lived who was killed a few days ago," of Francis Trench regularly attracting up to 150 people on the streets of Reading over a six-month period, and of John Molyneux's crowd of over eight hundred on Good Friday in Sudbury, many of whom reportedly went on to the regular services in church. Joseph Bardsley reported beginning work in a district in south east London with five hearers under a railway arch. Soon he had acquired an old sawmill and converted it into a place of worship, which, by 1864 was

> literally packed on Sundays by a congregation of six hundred to seven hundred poor people, the vast majority of whom never before were . . . found in the house of God. There are 120 communicants who month after month go on a Sunday evening to the parish church after their own service to receive the Holy Communion.[10]

There were a few on the episcopal bench who supported this kind of effort. Among them were C. R. Sumner of Winchester and A. C. Tait who, as bishop of London, himself engaged extensively in open air preaching in 1857.[11]

Churchmen outside the Evangelical party were often less than enthusiastic about irregular services. Aware of the need to attract the poor, some refrained from outright condemnation of street preaching, but preferred to use cathedral naves for popular services. Others looked upon open air preaching as a "regrettable necessity" to be tolerated only as long as pew rents effectively excluded most of the working class.[12] No such restraint hampered the old-fashioned high churchman J. W. Burgon who was horrified by any liturgical innovations; he denounced the "quasi-irregularities" of cottage lectures and "fancy services in a school room." Although Harry Jones found that the whole notion of special services for the poor had a "patronizing and uncomplimentary smell about it," yet he disliked even more the inelasticity of the formal system which confined the public worship of the church to regular services and limited preaching to regular sermons. Preaching in theaters, he thought, had "a smack of attractive incongruity" about it which "makes me suspect that the people who go one week to hear a sermon in a theatre would come the next to see a play in church." Furthermore, from the strictly professional point of view, he thought street preaching had much to be said for it:

> A course of unprotected sermons would do many a sheltered

preacher good. Let him step out of the system of revolving clerks, vergers and pew openers, of which he is the sun, and try to say a few words about the kingdom of heaven to the "masses" of whom we hear so much.[13]

Although enjoined in the Prayer Book the custom of reading daily morning and evening prayer had virtually died out in the parish churches of England by the end of the eighteenth century, and no significant revival of daily services took place until the Oxford Movement of the 1830s.[14] Often associated thereafter with Tractarian or high church views, nevertheless enthusiasm for the daily office was shared by writers of other persuasions. The liberal-minded John Sandford and Harry Jones supported the practice of daily services, and during the 1860s the Evangelical William Cadman instituted such services in his own parish of Marylebone. By 1870 the practice had spread widely. In his *Directorium Pastorale*, J. H. Blunt calculated that morning and evening prayer had been said in only three parish churches in England in 1840. By 1864 there were thirty-six such churches in London alone, and an additional twenty-eight in which one daily service was held. When the third edition of the *Directorium* appeared in 1872, 135 churches in London had daily services. In 1864 Blunt thought that about a thousand churches were "open daily for public prayer throughout England"; by 1872 his estimate had increased to sixteen hundred.[15]

Daily services were said to benefit three groups of people: the clergy themselves, their congregations, and the majority of parishioners who were unable or unwilling to attend.

For the clergy the daily offices were useful disciplines, precise obligations which could serve as a framework for their extraordinarily independent lives. They afforded the pastor continual opportunities for scripture reading and study, daily occasions for intercession, and a continual reminder of his unity with the whole church.[16] Parishioners who were faithful at daily services were promised secular as well as spiritual benefits. Edward Monro thought the services provided opportunities for the poor to escape the noise and crowd of their small cottages into an atmosphere of space and peacefulness, where reflection was possible. According to John Sandford, regularity at worship induced regularity in the ordinary work of those who made up the congregation, resulting in "greater economy of time . . . more punctuality and despatch in business . . . self-possession and serenity of mind . . . improved physical and moral health." Furthermore the ringing of the church bells, morning and night, reminded all parishioners, churchmen or not, "that religion should have a place in daily life."[17]

Daily morning and evening prayer did not attract great crowds of worshippers in mid-Victorian parishes. In the early 1840s John Sandford gathered an average of forty people for his morning service at Dunchurch, a parish of over thirteen hundred in 1848. A priest in a rural parish of 450 people claimed that his weekday adult congregations varied from a dozen to thirty in the 1850s.[18] Urban parishes fared less well. The rector of Bradford, for example, with a church which would accommodate about fourteen hundred people had a congregation of under twenty at his daily morning services, although he did ten times better at a regular Wednesday evening service with a sermon. Harry Jones wrote of services at St. Luke's, Berwick Street (where he was vicar from 1858 to 1872), at which only two or three laymen were present. According to Edward Monro one reason for the non-attendance of many working people in town and country was the insensitivity of clergy who set hours of services between 7:00 A.M. and 7:00 P.M. when only the well-to-do, and the aged and children among the poor were free to be present. This schedule created the unfortunate impression "that the clergy . . . have calls in the evening superior in their minds to the spiritual good of the poor."[19]

Preaching was clearly the main ingredient in the ordinary professional activity of Evangelical parsons; in the words of Ashton Oxenden it was the "prime duty . . . second to none." Yet the sermon was not neglected by pastoral theologians of other Anglican traditions either. The broad churchman Harry Jones considered it "difficult to overrate the value of preaching" and he devoted about one-fifth of his *Priest and Parish* to the problems of sermon composition and delivery. Although the Tractarian Edward Monro thought of sermons principally as bait to lead the poor to the sacraments and daily prayer, yet he rejected the tendency of his fellow Anglo-Catholics to undervalue preaching. In his *Parochial Work* he laid great stress on the need for frequent, plain, extemporaneous sermons for the poor, "plain words" to express "plain ideas." J. W. Burgon, another high churchman, also considered the sermon a means to attract people to church rather than an end in itself, but he gave it much attention on this account.[20]

These writers (and many others) worried that the elevated social and educational background of most parsons, unmodified by formal homiletical training before ordination, prevented them from becoming effective preachers to simple people. Pastoral theologians exhorted young ordinands deliberately to develop the virtue of plain speech, a virtue allegedly found more often among Dissenting ministers and lawyers than among Church of England clergy. "The sermon that is readily apprehended and easily remembered is the best sermon," wrote W. W. Champneys in his *Parish Work*, an opinion shared by his fellow Evangelical J. C. Ryle who advised graduate clergy to throw away the sophistications of Oxford and Cambridge in order to be understood by the unlettered folk who occupied many pews.[21]

By the 1860s some writers were more concerned about reaching the educated élite than the ignorant masses. Lacking professional knowledge and professional skills, most incumbents were also thought to be ignorant of contemporary intellectual problems and controversies. Much preaching by many clergy innocent of any serious awareness of modern biblical studies and theology was no defense against rising scepticism and infidelity. The views of such clergymen were discounted by the educated public. They lost their positions as leaders of thought, and they were rendered incompetent to deal pastorally with those whose faith was unsettled.[22]

Pastoral handbook writers did more than offer general comment on preaching or deplore the low state of the sermon in the English church. They also provided precise direction on particular matters. This advice centered on three facets of the preaching art: choice of topic; method of preparation; manner of delivery.

Evangelicals thought that conversion was the proper aim of all preaching. High churchmen, on the other hand, taught that the art of the preacher was to persuade his hearers to participate in the community life of the church and to help them understand her doctrines.[23] Readers of Harry Jones's *Priest and Parish* found there a concept of the purpose of preaching which differed from that of either Evangelicals or high churchmen. According to Jones "the object of the preacher is not so much to save souls, or to destroy the works of the devil, as to promote that which does each of these things at once, i.e., promote truth and the love of it." The preacher's business, wrote this broad churchman, is to

> make the cobblers in his congregation patch with more care, and the children spell and sum with more pains . . . simply because it becomes a Christian child and a Christian cobbler to do his best.[24]

Although these differences in emphasis corresponded to different party views, handbook writers of all shades of churchmanship agreed on the main sources for sermon subjects: pastoral experience and the bible. The daily experience of visiting and pastoral care should play upon a consciousness steeped in prayer and reflection on the biblical writings.[25]

Many high church pastoral writers insisted that sound preaching demanded a heavy course of theological reading in addition to bible study. J. J. Blunt, for example, devoted three of the eleven chapters in his *Duties of the Parish Priest* to the amount and type of reading he thought necessary. The required works constituted a substantial list, including the church fathers of the first five centuries in the original languages as well as the "original authorities" of the English Reformation. With all this stored in his mind the priest might safely turn to modern works if he found any extra time.[26] Although Blunt's emphasis on antiquity was rather extreme, most other high church writers agreed that the priest's reading should consist chiefly of the bible and patristic theology, and should exclude what Wilberforce described as "carnal and worldly studies." This rigorous high church regime was designed to do more than guarantee orthodox preaching. The study of early theological disputes was undertaken to equip the priest as a religious specialist, to give him the academic tools to cope with contemporary heresies in a professional way. "What is thought of a lawyer who cannot form and give an opinion on a case?" asked H. R. Lloyd,

> or of a physician who cannot recognize disease? . . . or of a commander . . . who cannot . . . make his dispositions? . . . In like manner what is the use of an unlearned unmeditative priest . . . who cannot think accurately nor express readily and clearly what is reasonable and just and true concerning a

question of conscience, or of any other religous point asked him unexpectedly by a parishioner?[27]

Neither Evangelicals nor broad churchmen followed the high church line about professional reading. Such Evangelical pastoral writers as Charles Bridges and Ashton Oxenden never positively rejected extra-biblical theological study. But they worried lest it should occupy time better spent on practical pastoral work, and they feared that "every enlargement of intellectual knowledge has a natural tendency to self-exaltation."[28] Harry Jones, on the other hand, recommended just those works which Samuel Wilberforce thought "carnal and worldly." Jones was dubious about the value of a "ministry of laborious and precise theologians," and he felt that priests gained little from "writers who are severely professional." Instead parish priests should read widely, so equipping themselves for contemporary (not ancient) intellectual challenges. Jones advised the clergyman to search out "large-hearted books" and the works of "respectable heretics," the latter to be read "without any feverish anxiety about the stability of the truth." He showed no interest in increasing the sort of specialized knowledge which would mark the priest off from other educated men.[29]

Handbook authors had much to say to preachers about the technique of preparation and delivery. The preacher should prepare a plan which would allow for the "clear arrangement of . . . subject matter."[30] That matter itself should be limited, for the sermon must have unity and make a single main point. Nearly all the pastoral theologians worried lest preachers go on too long, although their conception of the optimum sermon length varied considerably. Most writers had a horror of homiletic jargon, of "new fangled words such as 'prayerful'" or "the stereotype repeated 'brethren.'"[31] Although they should shun ferocious exhortation preachers must also studiously avoid pandering to the prejudices of the congregation. Words must be distinctly enunciated in a natural voice, and the preacher's throat deserved careful attention.[32]

Extemporaneous preaching was a matter for some discussion. The freer style was often considered to be particularly suitable for congregations of the poor, whereas the polish of written discourses was thought to be preferred by the superior classes.[33] Views on the comparative merits or usefulness of extemporaneous and

43

written sermons did not correspond to the lines of churchmanship. Preaching without a text appealed to many Evangelicals; yet W. W. Champneys stressed the advantages of accurate order and controlled length which derived from the discipline of preparing a manuscript. On the other hand, Edward Monro and William Sewell, both Anglo-Catholics, favored the warmth and naturalness of the extemporaneous approach.[34] Most handbook authors advised pastors to be prepared to preach either way, and they warned clergy that extemporaneous preaching required highly disciplined preparation.[35] In fact careful thought and hard work before preaching could only be avoided by buying or borrowing the sermons of others, practices unworthy of a professional man of God. Homiletical plagiarism declined in the nineteenth century and the once thriving trade in manuscript sermons was brought into disrepute. In 1869 the *Guardian* refused to accept advertisements of manuscript sermons for sale.[36]

Sections of pastoral handbooks dealing with the sacraments are remarkably free of the acrimony usually associated with theological and liturgical wrangling over baptism and the eucharist in the nineteenth-century church. Their authors' aims were directly pastoral; for the most part decidedly practical and professional.

Handbook authors found an appalling ignorance of the nature of baptism among laymen, and especially among the poor. "I have actually found old women (nurses and midwives) confuse Baptism and vaccination," wrote J. H. Blunt in 1864. Dubious motives often caused the poor to bring their babies to the font, the most common being a natural desire to collect money from burial clubs that would pay only for the funerals of baptized infants.[37] To raise the level of popular understanding and to make more effective pastoral use of the sacrament, handbook writers (of widely differing churchmanship) urged the clergy to give careful attention to the choice of sponsors and the instruction of parents. One clerical meeting even suggested that special groups of devout communicants should be formed in each parish to sponsor illegitimate children born in workhouses.[38] Whenever possible the rite should be performed publicly in church. The service itself should be "a sermon to the eye and ear" of the congregation, and the pastor might use the occasion to teach his whole flock about Christian initiation.[39] This sort of careful instruction and individual pastoral care may have been feasible in rural or small town parishes, but it must have been utterly impossible in the depths of the great cities of the 1850s and 1860s, where the clergy were kept busy mechanically administering the sacrament of baptism.[40]

Just as adult Christians were to be made conscious of their responsibility as sponsors and aware of the meaning of baptism, so teenagers were to be fostered morally and prepared intellectually before confirmation. Confirmation services themselves were episcopal, not parochial, responsibilities. Until the railway made travel easy in the early Victorian years, occasions for confirmation had been relatively few. In the eighteenth century a conscientious bishop would normally confirm triennially as part of his regular visitation; huge numbers were brought from a wide area to the chosen center.[41] From the 1830s on, confirmation services were held more frequently in more places. Fewer candidates were presented each time and consequently the services were more reverent and orderly.

Order and discipline were problems throughout the period of preparation which was increasingly considered mandatory before the candidates were presented to the bishop. Clergy attempted to instruct confirmation candidates at just that period in their lives when they were most unmanageable and recalcitrant, between the ages of fifteen and eighteen.[42] Removed from the imposed disciplines of day school and Sunday school they often took work which uprooted them from the parental home at the period when they were most subject to "the perplexities which arise out of the deep workings of our corrupt nature."[43] John Sandford thought that most adolescents regarded clergymen and schoolmasters as their "natural enemies." Certainly the middle teens were years when young people fell away from the church. To demonstrate this one Lancashire Sunday school teacher in the 1860s traced one hundred of his old pupils; he discovered that only two continued to attend a place of worship.[44]

Despite these difficulties, pastoral theologians argued the importance both of group teaching and of individual guidance for teen-age confirmation candidates before they were presented to the bishop. Group sessions were designed to increase the young person's religious knowledge and his appreciation of Christian duty. The aim of the individual interviews was moral: to examine, inform, and sensitize each candidate's conscience.

Most handbook writers favored special confirmation classes

lasting from five weeks to three months, and meeting at least weekly during that period.[45] The instructing priest was advised to take careful note of the names, ages, and progress of each candidate. J. H. Blunt thought the course should be based on the Prayer Book and should include "systematic instruction in Faith, Duty, and the subject of Confirmation" as well as the doctrine of Holy Communion and "habits of prayer and self-examination." W. W. Champneys included a complete outline of lessons in his *Parish Work*, and both he and J. H. Blunt used the device of the take-home examination to test the results of their pedagogical efforts. Sometimes the teaching methods recommended by the handbook writers were less than gentle. J. W. Burgon insisted that all potential candidates be dragooned to class, the "hopeless ones" as well as the "docile children" of the parish. Having cajoled, persuaded, and ordered as many as possible to meet with him, the pastor must then do almost anything to keep the class together:

> He may strike the table with his clenched fist if he can procure attention in no more scientific way, while he pours out before them some plain truths about Death and Judgement, Heaven and Hell—in the most idiomatic English he can command.[46]

One traditional means of group instruction was the catechetical method, a dialogue of questions and answers on matters of faith and doctrine described by Charles Bridges as "pumping knowledge into the children and then pumping it out again." This practice had continued (although in a rather restricted form) throughout the dim period of the late eighteenth century, and it was favored by a number of Victorian pastoral writers as a Sunday evening alternative to the ordinary sermon and as a suitable form of direct clerical participation in the teaching of parochial day schools.[47]

Burgon thought that about ten percent of a parish should be in course of preparation for confirmation at any one time. Whether or not this was reasonable at his own parish of St. Mary's in Oxford, it would have been an impossible ideal for urban clergy in overpopulated districts. Nevertheless it is remarkable how much teaching of this sort did go on in cities. In 1840, Walter Hook personally prepared 256 candidates for confirmation. In T. J. Rowsell's enormous parish of St. Peter's, Stepney, a group of 112 candidates was taken through a three-month course in 1857. After seeing each young person individually, Rowsell met the whole group as a class every Sunday after the evening service, and often on Wednesdays and Fridays as well. On Sunday nights, when he asked parents and other interested adults to remain for the instruction, he found that six or seven hundred normally did so.[48]

Most pastoral writers considered individual conversations with each confirmation candidate quite as important as group instruction. Burgon recommended at least two private interviews, one when a youth came forward for instruction, and a second, about fifteen minutes in length, just before the service itself. The Evangelical W. W. Champneys saw each candidate privately after he had administered an examination on the work covered in classes, and the high churchman Walsham How thought that the private interviews at which he examined the candidates' prayer life were "at once the most laborious and the most blessed portion of all his private ministrations."[49]

Once confirmed, the communicant youth needed continual encouragement along the way of faith and good conduct. This was provided to him through the agencies of evening schools, bible classes, and parochial club life, as well as by involving him in the work of Sunday school teaching. Champneys asked those who were confirmed to sign their names in a record book every time they attended Holy Communion. Burgon recommended yet another private interview with each new communicant one year after confirmation, and Walsham How thought that such interviews should be repeated from time to time and should form a continuing part of the clergyman's pastoral work.[50]

Opportunities for the newly confirmed to receive the Holy Communion were steadily increasing in the English church during the first half of the nineteenth century. In the eighteenth century and the early years of the nineteenth century the parochial norm was a celebration four times a year: at Christmas, Easter, Whitsunday (Pentecost), and once in the autumn. Yet even in the eighteenth century there were more occasions than this in some parishes. On the other hand the quarterly pattern persisted in many rural parishes as late as the 1860s. Despite these exceptions, by the 1850s monthly communion was usual, and more frequent celebrations had become quite common. This change can be traced to Evangelical seriousness as well as to Tractarian sacramentalism. During the fifties and sixties the sacrament was celebrated weekly in parishes of both types, and emphasis on eucharistic worship is to be found in writers of both traditions.[51]

Furthermore both Evangelical and high church pastoral theologians recommended that each parish priest nurture a group of devout communicants which should meet regularly for prayer and scripture reading. Such a group was to be the nucleus of the parish; its members would become what Oxenden called a "valuable staff" to aid the parish priest. According to Burgon this clutch of the committed would serve both to extend the Church's ministry in the parish and also as an appropriate audience for the parson to convey "a large amount of Christian instruction without the formality of the pulpit." Its members would form a suitable pool of sponsors for baptism.[52] Such devoted churchmen would value the services of their ordained professional religious advisers, through whom they had access to spiritual and theological resources not sought by ordinary members of the national church. The pastor, in turn/ often found it rewarding to work especially for those who appreciated the benefits of his expertise. As one participant in a clerical meeting put it, "God's glory is promoted more by the increasing sanctification of the few than by making a certain impression on the many." This concentration of ministry on the pious few, with its emphasis on the worthy reception of the sacrament, did not appeal to such liberal characters as the old Oxford noetic, Archbishop Richard Whately. He warned against religious élitism, against the notion that the Holy Communion "is designed for those only who have attained to a certain perfection in holiness beyond what is required of Christians generally."[53]

According to the handbook writers, a priest's public ministry would be effective only if he knew his parishioners as individuals. Effective preaching presupposed knowledge of the concerns and capacities of one's hearers; candidates were to be prepared for confirmation by individual interview as well as by group instruction; select communicant groups were advocated by some as means of retaining this close contact after confirmation. Ministry to individuals was, however, more than an adjunct of public ministry. It had importance and purposes of its own which were stressed by writers of all schools of thought.

Although both Evangelical and liberal churchmen were fully conscious of this side of pastoral care, those in the high church and Tractarian traditions gave it particular emphasis. They felt that dealing with parishioners only in masses or even small groups was simply ineffective. "Men of the most different stages and degrees of holiness," stated a writer in the *Christian Remembrancer* in 1845, "the most contrary traits of character, [too often] are all treated with the same method and have the same medicine administered, although what is life to the one is positive poison to the other." To avoid this error the clergyman should function very like a doctor; he must "obtain the same intimate acquaintance with the souls of individuals which the physician obtains of their bodies."[54] He required certain gifts of character, notably sympathy, caution, and common sense; but he also needed to cultivate the art of casuistry and the capacity to listen. Further, he must know the shape of his parish: its social and economic life, its customs and the patterns of conduct of its denizens. Only when he really knew the secular life of his parish could he cope with the cure of souls of its inhabitants.[55]

An observant and sensitive pastor would use personal and family crises, as well as special occasions and celebrations, to draw his individual parishioners more fully under his care. A marriage was one such opportunity. Although the clerical monopoly of marriage ended in 1836, and the relative percentage of marriage ceremonies performed in parish churches thereafter declined, the huge majority continued to be celebrated in the national church, and in some urban churches the number of weddings reached enormous proportions. Each was an occasion for the priest to develop a continuing pastoral relationship.[56]

Burials provided even greater opportunities. When a mourner's heart was softened by grief, the sensitive pastor might win his soul and so establish contact with a family hitherto unconnected with the church. J. W. Burgon found that alienated members of bereaved families could be drawn together by a skillful priest:

A reconciliation which before seemed impracticable may be effected now. Two brothers may be persuaded to shake hands over a parent's grave. . . . This is ministerial work! This is to shepherd a flock!

Some clergy attempted to use death as an occasion for discipline by refusing to use the Prayer Book service to bury those who had been notoriously immoral or infidels. One pastorally unfortunate effect of the Cemetery Acts of 1852 and 1853, which required the closure of crowded town and city churchyards and burial in cemeteries outside the urban areas, was the disconnection of parishioner and priest at the time of death. In such cases the burial office was performed by a cemetery chaplain, and, except by chance, the parish priest knew nothing of the death at all.[57]

Important as it was to exploit domestic crises when they arose, a conscientious pastor would often find it necessary to create his own opportunities in order to establish personal relationships with members of his flock. He could do this either by encourageing his people to come to him, or by himself visiting them.

On 5 February 1846 the Alcester Clerical Meeting held a discussion on the subject of "pastoral intercourse with individuals," especially "labouring men and farm or other domestic servants" who were difficult to meet on regular parish visits. The meeting concluded that parishioners of this class must be invited to call on their pastors by appointment. Edward Monro made a similar suggestion. He recommended that an incumbent with an agricultural parish of about one thousand souls should devote three hours on three days every week to such interviews, each to be about fifteen minutes in length. "This habit of seeing our people individually," wrote Monro,

> would be with a view to bringing them to feel the need of giving us their fuller confidence in the confession of sins with which they are burdened.[58]

The practice of private confession was identified with the Tractarian leaders, and in the 1850s became the focus of acrimonious partisan disputes. Monro was an Anglo-Catholic, although a moderate one, and it is hardly surprising that he should approve of private confession. Nor is it an unexpected discovery that Walsham How, an Anglo-Catholic pastoral writer of the next generation, argued that this function was "possibly the most important of the private ministrations of the parish priest."[59] In fact private confession in the English church was neither entirely a

Tractarian revival nor wholly an Anglo-Catholic enthusiasm. Although the twenty-fifth of the Thirty-Nine Articles denied penance the status of a sacrament, nevertheless the Prayer Book clearly recommended private absolution for any who could not otherwise quiet their consciences in preparation for Holy Communion, and it provided for special confession and absolution in the Order for the Visitation of the Sick. No doubt these provisions were generally neglected at the beginning of the nineteenth century. But the neglect was not complete. Three years before the Oxford Movement began, Henry Thompson, the author of *Pastoralia*, specifically advised his clerical readers to encourage the sick to make special confession, and in the very year of Keble's assize sermon, Samuel Wilberforce, in his *Notebook of a Country Clergyman*, raised the classic pastoral problem of whether a priest should ever reveal the secrets of a confession for the public good.[60]

Later in the century, when the confessional had become a focus of party warfare, moderate high church writers still recommended the limited use of private confession in the Prayer Book tradition. Wilberforce himself produced a classic statement of the Anglican position and its pastoral usefulness, and J. W. Burgon emphasized the need to deal with sin directly and effectively when visiting the sick, although he did not consider that formal absolution was always necessary. The most detailed professional advice to pastors was provided by J. H. Blunt. In his *Directorium Pastorale* he observed that "many holy, far-sighted and experienced clergymen look upon [confession] as a valuable part of the pastor's work," and he pointed out that "almost all zealous clergymen of the Evangelical school" encouraged this practice, although they substituted a prayer for pardon or conversion for absolution. Not part of her pastoral system nor essential to salvation, private confession was nevertheless a legitimate form of individual relationship between parishioner and pastor in the Church of England. A clergyman was always bound to receive confessions if volunteered, and, wrote Blunt, "under particular specified circumstances" actually to encourage his parishioners to confess their sins. He added that clergy must not only observe the seal of the confessional scrupulously, but must also regard as privileged all "communications made to them not manifestly of an open kind."[61]

Private confession had a very limited appeal to Anglican laymen and formed a very small part of the pastoral ministry of the

Church of England to individuals. In contrast, parish visiting was universally recognised as an important element in the ministry of every incumbent. Some pastoral theologians explicitly acknowledged secular reasons for parish visiting, especially among the poor. R. W. Evans thought that, as "the only person in the parish that is concerned to understand all its relations and affairs" the conscientious visiting parson could become "a most useful source of information to the ruling powers." Henry Mackenzie, while incumbent of St. Martin's-in-the-Fields, suggested an unusually explicit form of church and state alliance at the parochial level, a "system of home visitation under the joint direction of the clergyman of the parish, the chairman of the Board of Guardians, and the District Inspector of Police", with a view to rationalizing the distribution of charity. By means of such joint action, Mackenzie thought that "the great legal power of the Magistrate and the Poor Law Commissioner would be hallowed and sanctified and brought into immediate relationship with the great moral power of the ministry of the Gospel of Christ."[62] By others the house call was seen as a means of injecting a higher culture into the lives of the poor as well as a vehicle of reconciliation among different social classes. The clergyman's visit was frequently an occasion for performing many minor offices:

> "You may sign pay-warrants or club-certificates; you may read, or perhaps write a letter, or explain the whereabouts of the son's regiment in foreign parts; or help some poor girl . . . to follow her husband who had gone off with the recruiting-sergeant." A ticket for a dispensary, a good word to the Board of Guardians, or an order for a parish coffin, may all become an earnest of good will.[63]

Important as were these secular elements in pastoral visiting, Victorian handbook authors considered them mere by-products of a priest's sacred duty to seek out the individual children of God, to stand between them and their Maker.

The first responsibility of the visiting priest was to his sick parishioners, and the purpose of visiting the sick was to prepare them for death. Even minor illness was seen as a reminder of mortality, a chance for reflection on the immediacy of heavenly judgement, an opportunity for moral accounting. Mortal illness gave the victim time to prepare for his own personal confrontation with God; and it was the clergyman's task to assist in this preparation. Ailing unbelievers or backsliders must be brought to repentance, to awareness of their plight, and so put in the way of rescue by the loving Redeemer.[64]

The certainty and nearness of death, and the awful prospect of meeting God face to face, were vivid realities to Victorian pastoral writers. Times of sickness were seen as a clergyman's best opportunity to awaken and to strengthen consciousness of these realities among his people. Although the priest's manner when visiting the sick should always be kind and cheerful, yet, wrote Harry Jones, "it is part of his business to tell you that sickness is the symptom of death," dark tidings, no doubt, although "the brightest daylight lies beyond." Fear of infection must never be allowed to prevent a pastor from delivering this message. It was his duty to care for the sick man's soul just as it was the duty of the physician to care for the sick man's body. Like a physician, the priest must always enter the sick man's room; yet he, like the doctor, should take all reasonable precautions to avoid infection while he is there.[65]

Sensitivity and thoughtfulness were key factors in the clergyman's approach to the sick. It was important to keep in mind the tastes and characters of the people he was visiting and always to show a proper respect for their dignity. Oxenden wrote that the pastor should never be intrusive, never enter a poor man's house without removing his hat and showing every courtesy expected of a visitor. With wonderful condescension Burgon wrote of the poor that

> their feelings are quite as acute as ours. They do not indeed feel *what* we feel; but they feel *as* we do. They have a code of their own, which there is no danger of violating if we be but sincerely desirous not to hurt their feelings.

Friendliness ("kind looks, gentle tones, loving words," as Champneys described it) was important in gaining the patient's confidence. The patient must be seen alone, and the visitor's first aim should be what J. H. Blunt described as a "kind of pastoral diagnosis." Following this common medical analogy Wilberforce wrote that the priest's examination was like that of "the courageous surgeon who probes to the very bottom of the wound which he would cure." J. H. Blunt recommended careful listing of sick parishioners, both as to the nature of their physical condition ("infirm and aged"; "temporary sickness"; "mortal sickness or . . . long lingering decline") and according to their relationship to the Christian faith ("church people"; "Dissenters"; "indifferent").[66] Different conditions required different therapies. Many writers felt the formal Prayer Book visitation office appropriate only for committed church people, and urged that the parson be given freedom to select suitable prayers and scripture readings, or to do without forms at all. By one means or another all must be brought to self-examination and repentance, and the priest must be prepared to cope with the reality of sin, avoiding what Burgon described as either "a morbid unwillingness to approach the subject" or "an inquisitorial officiousness." It was his duty, wrote Harry Jones, to "treat sin as a disease and be no more horrified and shocked at it than the doctor is at the bruise or the cut, though they be deserved." Holy Communion should be available to the faithful, but the sacrament should be guarded carefully against misinterpretation and misuse by the ignorant and the superstitious.[67]

Although frequent calls on the sick were a very special duty (Oxenden said they should be seen at least once a week; Monro thought terminal cases should be visited daily), regular house-to-house visitation of all the families and individual residents of the parish was also considered by most pastoral writers to be an essential part of the sacred ministry. One purpose for such visits was to encourage parishioners to attend church services. Regular visiting was thought to build up the spiritual society of the church and to break down those secular social barriers which too often inhibited a priest's ministry. How could a parson know his people, and so minister effectively in the pulpit or at the sick-bed unless he knew where they lived and worked? How could he deal with moral wickedness or error if he confined his ministry to the church building, or to the faithful? He must cope directly with Dissenters and sceptics, and seek out the agents of immorality around him, dealing, wrote J. H. Blunt, with persons "who are, most frequently, unconscious of their malady."[68]

Among the personal qualities essential to the successful home visitor the capacity to plan carefully and the ability to work methodically were prominent. Bishop Wilberforce expected the pastor to work with the aid of a map, and to plan a round of visitations so that every part of his flock would be seen in a regular course. He should set an objective, a particular number of visits that he intended to make each week. The frequency of visits recommended by different pastoral theologians varied from monthly to yearly, but all handbook writers agreed that the important things were regularity and system. A useful aid in all this was a parish visiting register or pastoral diary, in which the priest could maintain up-to-date information about the religious and secular condition of each family. By thus keeping track of his people he would always be aware of special situations when he entered particular houses; his visits would have distinct aims and be more likely to fulfill definite needs.[69]

The great obstacle to universal home visiting (in fact to realizing the ideal of a personal ministry to every member of every parish in any way) was the massive growth in England's population during the first half of the nineteenth century. In most urban parishes the people were simply too many to be cared for in the traditional way by the relatively small number of clergy available. "There never was such a strain upon the territorial system of any organized church in the history of the world," bemoaned J. Bardsley at the church congress of 1865. Harry Jones, who was a London pastor himself, wrote of the overwhelming "sense of work untouched," of the "paralysing pressure of unattained results [which] weighs a sensitive man down until he almost drops." Often the only resident gentleman in a squalid slum, the town clergyman was abandoned too frequently to his fate, forgotten by the purveyors of church patronage. "They come up full of zeal from the universities," wrote a contributor to the *Quarterly Review*,

> many of them young, not a few men of considerable mark; they fling themselves into the missionary undertaking, as they call it, and in less than six months, from the absence of all sympathy and all results, they become broken-hearted.[70]

As early as 1838 H. W. Wilberforce called the parish system "wholly obsolete" in urban areas. Later on, Lord Shaftesbury, Walter Hook, and James Fraser came to much the same conclusion, and each recommended that the church find other methods of ministry in cities.[71] Most churchmen, however, sought to adjust the old system to the new environment, to streamline the machinery rather than to replace it. Two particularly important types of adjustment were proposed to render the traditional parish organization of the church appropriate to urban conditions. One type consisted of attempts to reorganize both the structure and the ordained staff of large parishes to allow for more efficient pastoral care; the other included a variety of efforts to share the sacred duties of the clergy with select bands of devout lay people. As these innovations spread they brought with them an important change in the function of the clergy themselves: increasingly urban clergy became administrators of the religious machinery of their parishes rather than ministers to their flocks.

The first effort at structural change was to create new districts within unmanageably large parishes, to build new church buildings, and to establish independent pastoral units. Parliament was involved in this movement from the time of the Church Building Act of 1818 to Sir Robert Peel's District Churches Act of 1843. The early grants of money to the church building commission for church construction proved politically impossible to continue as the Dissenting community gained in power and self-consciousness in the second quarter of the century. The funds made available by loan to the ecclesiastical commissioners by Peel's Act in 1843 were insufficient to provide for the independent support of clergy in all the districts needing intensive pastoral care. Nevertheless, much was done by the Ecclesiastical Commission, and much more by private benefaction. By 1863, three hundred new parishes had been endowed and many other benefices in large towns augmented with the assistance of the commission; between 1840 and 1876, 1,727 new churches were built in England and Wales.[72] This policy of parochial division seemed obvious to many in the 1850s and 1860s who sought to recreate the close personal contact between pastor and people which, as we have seen, was basic to the pastoral ideal of the English church. Parish subdivision provided for that independence of action traditionally enjoyed by the parish priest, and it allowed for the development of a healthy local loyalty among the laity.[73]

By the middle decades of the century this policy had vigorous opponents among the active urban parochial clergy. These critics insisted that centralization rather than division was a better strategy for effective pastoral care in large towns. Supporters of centralization pointed to the financial impossibility of providing a sound material base for all the new independent districts required if the policy of division was to work effectively. Some also felt that subdivision contributed to the isolation of the poor in particular urban districts, a development which Abraham Hume of Liverpool noted was occurring anyway as the rich left the downtown districts to make their homes in salubrious suburbs. To disadvantages like inadequate financial resources and social divisiveness others added the isolation of clergy in difficult slum areas.[74] All these reasons led such London clergy as Bryan King of St. Georges-in-the-East, John Kempe of St. James, Charles Eyre of Marylebone, Henry Mackenzie of St. Martin-in-the-Fields, and, above all, William Cadman of Southwark, to argue strongly in favor of retaining single parish units, often with tens of thousands of inhabitants each. They all agreed with Cadman that effective individual pastoral care could be provided in such a parish by a staff of efficiently organized curates working under the direction of a single "presiding clergyman."[75]

As Cadman described his own practice in papers and speeches given at church congresses in the 1860s, he developed a coherent theory of centralized ministry. St. George's, Southwark, of which he was the incumbent from 1852 until 1869, contained thirty thousand inhabitants, most of whom were very poor indeed. The parish church could accommodate one thousand people, yet only twenty-five of his thirty thousand parishioners showed up on Cadman's first Sunday. Immediately after his arrival he divided the parish for pastoral purposes into six districts of about five thousand inhabitants. A curate, assisted by lay helpers, was placed in charge of each of these. In his subdivision the district curate attempted to reproduce the work of the parish church, including preaching, schooling, and home visiting. The curate's first task was to find or construct a building in the local district which could be used as a school as well as a place of worship:

> It may be an upper room over some workshop, or an iron church in an unoccupied yard, or an house with partitions between two rooms taken down. . . . A coachhouse and stables may be thrown together.

The mother church, however, remained the center of the whole parish. Each of the curates continued to assist in its worship, and each occasionally held a special service there for the people from his own district. The rector took upon himself "pecuniary responsibility" for the whole parish so that the assistant curate might carry on without "withdrawal from pastoral work by necessary solicitations . . . for the salary of his teachers, for the building of his schools, for the expenses of his church." The curates had the advantage of professional supervision by a mature experienced pastor.[76]

Cadman's address to the 1863 church congress was significantly entitled "Management of a Large Parish." "Management requires a manager," stated Cadman, "one who seeks that wisdom which is 'profitable to direct.'" He was not the only clergyman to recognize the importance of administrative competence in the parish priest. Charles Bridges thought it the task of parish ministers "to set many lesser wheels in motion in subservient harmony with the grand movements of the machine." Harry Jones had a good deal to say about "management or generalship in parochial economies," and Henry Mackenzie pointed to the value of this quality in the ministers of scattered rural parishes. No one was clearer about the importance of administrative talent and skill than Robert Gregory, a man with extensive urban pastoral experience in Lambeth. He was convinced that the main task of the chief minister in a large city was the development and supervision of a staff. For the incumbent himself to "toil night and day at visiting the sick, relieving the distressed, teaching in the schools, managing clubs [and] conducting charitable institutions" was positively bad, for it prevented his consideration of total strategy. It was comparable to a general who insisted on "mounting guard, conducting forays, leading charges in his own person." The chief pastor's proper task was to recruit, to train, and to supervise a staff of suitable people, clerical and lay, male and female, through whom he could carry on the total ministry of the parish. The "first care" of the priest should be these fellow workers. As the "centre around which they are to be collected" he should provide continual oversight, firm but also sensitive to the feelings and ideas of his subordinates. He should not be an autocrat

who is simply to assign tasks to his coadjutors. His plans . . .

should be introduced as schemes to be discussed, not as decisions that have been arrived at. All should be encouraged to comment upon what is proposed that all may feel an interest in whatever is undertaken. . . . Those who are working with him are cooperating friends, not ductile dependents.[77]

Gregory and Cadman were both quite clear that the pastoral care of large urban parishes required not only subordinate clergy but lay helpers as well. Some Anglo-Catholic clergymen worried that lay ministers might infringe on territory which belonged to the pastoral profession alone. R. M. Benson, the founder of the Cowley fathers, for example, had no use for parochial lay assistants at all. He believed that the whole work of the church was "the distribution and maintenance of spiritual life," a work for the clergy alone "with which the people have properly nothing to do." Similar though rather less extreme opinions appeared in the columns of the *Christian Remembrancer*. Evangelicals were not clerical monopolists, and even moderate high church pastoral theologians admitted the desirability of lay help especially in urban parishes. The common phrase "lay cooperation" could mean, of course, many things. J. H. Blunt considered all sorts of topics under this head: the office of church warden; church singing; money raising; teaching and lecturing in Sunday schools and evening classes; and the distribution of alms. Others were concerned that laymen have an effective voice in the consultative and policy making life of the church. The most urgent need, however, was for visitors, for men and women to make personal contact between the local parish church and the poor.[78]

To fill this need two main sorts of lay agent emerged in the period from 1830 to 1870: paid full-time lay helpers and volunteer "district visitors." The Sisters of Mercy constituted a third type, generally preferred by Anglo-Catholics. Although some work was done by the sisters in urban districts (for example in Bryan King's parish of St. George's-in-the-East) popular anti-Catholicism and the impractical romanticism of many of the early Anglican attempts to re-establish the religious life prevented the movement from expanding widely. An order of deaconesses, the evangelical parallel to Sisters of Mercy, was proposed in the 1850s, and the North London Deaconess Institution was opened in the early 1860s; but in 1863 only three deaconesses were actually at work.[79]

Paid full-time lay helpers went by different names; the most common were scripture readers, bible women, and parochial mission women. Nearly all the agents were themselves of social classes only slightly, if at all, above the urban poor among whom they were sent to minister. Although sometimes supported entirely by local parishes, they were often supplied and paid by outside bodies, most of them Evangelical agencies. Of these agencies the most suspect among high churchmen was the non-denominational London City Mission, governed by a committee made up equally of Dissenters and Evangelical churchmen. Founded in 1835, it was a substantial organization which deployed 375 agents in 1860 and over 450 by the early 1880s. Although willing to place its agents under the supervision of cooperative incumbents, the City Mission was quite prepared to allow them to carry out house-to-house visits, as well as to lead prayers, hold bible meetings, and preach on the streets in parishes where the clergy opposed their efforts. Such lack of respect for established authority made high churchmen like Robert Gregory furious. Although Gregory fully recognized the need for lay visitors, he had no use for City Missionaries who "dog the footsteps of the clergy" and "with an offensive pretence of neutrality . . . do their best to undermine the church's teaching." On the other hand many Evangelical London clergy accepted their services willingly; W. W. Champneys employed two in Whitechapel and William Cadman had four under his direction in Southwark.[80]

Less controversial sources of Evangelical lay helpers were the Church Pastoral Aid Society (founded in 1836) and the Church of England Scripture Readers' Association (established in 1844), whose agents were instructed always to work under the direction of the parochial clergy. Another variety of Evangelical lay assistant was the "bible woman" of whom there were said to be one hundred in London parishes in 1860. Similar, although high church rather than Evangelical, were the "Parochial Church Women" who were at work in ten London parishes in 1861. In order to get a full picture of the extent of help given by full-time lay helpers, numerous scripture readers recruited locally by parish priests would have to be added to all those sponsored and supported by external bodies. In the mid-fifties male scripture readers in London parishes were paid about seventy pounds, less by thirty pounds than the amount earned by assistant curates in the same or

60

similar situations. Women workers evidently received substantially lower stipends.[81]

Most clergy considered scripture readers to be very helpful as visitors among the poor as long as they remained under the control of the incumbent. Some clergymen, in fact, thought that one reader was worth two curates. Less expensive than assistant clergy, paid lay pastoral helpers often developed a long-term commitment to their neighborhoods undisturbed by the ambition to rise professionally which naturally affected assistantn curates. As laymen of very modest social standing they did not provoke the suspicion of parsons which commonly inhibited clerical visits to the homes of the poor. Described by Bishop Robert Bickersteth as "pioneers for the clergy amongst the most degraded parts of the population," they were thought to form a "connecting link between the clergyman and the poorest portion of his parishioners." Important sources of pastoral information to the clergy as well as of religious comfort to the sick poor, they extended individual pastoral care to numbers of people beyond the reach of parish priests and their curates. Many who placed great emphasis on the ideals of clerical character and gentility felt it was far better to share pastoral work with socially humble laymen than to increase the numbers of clergy by ordaining poorly educated nongentlemen as priests, deacons, or even subdeacons. A writer in the *Quarterly Review* noted that a layman was less likely to "compromise the character of the church" than a low type of cleric. He was also more likely to obtain a better "hearing among the profligate" than a man in orders, even if the orders were only those of a "subdeacon." Walter Hook pointed out that if a lay agent failed he could be relegated to a secular occupation, a course impossible in dealing with a failed clergyman, who, having acquired indelible ministerial character could not be assigned to non-ministerial work.[82]

More numerous than scripture readers and bible women, and even more widely welcomed by the clergy, were amateur lay workers known as district visitors. Two features distinguished these from paid pastoral helpers: they were volunteers; and they were generally drawn from the middle and upper classes. There are references to voluntary pastoral work by members of the working class. The knifegrinders of Leeds, for example, were "commissioned to seek out unbaptised children," and they report-

61

edly brought four hundred to the local clergy for christening. However district visiting was normally an occupation of the affluent and leisured, a personal ministry of the wealthy to the deprived. "Contact, and not distant gifts only," said T. J. Rowsell, "can create and convince of love." This meant more than contact between rich and poor within a single parish. It also involved developing personal relationships between Christians of different social classes who lived in geographically distinct sectors of cities and towns. Robert Gregory of Lambeth described the provision of visitors to his poor area as "the practical way in which 'the West End' has . . . stretched out a helping hand to this necessitous district."[83]

Few men apparently had time or inclination to engage in this work. But it was a popular activity for ladies. In 1850, for example, 13,000 visits were paid by ladies in the district of Park Chapel, Chelsea, and in 1859 female district visitors made 25,864 calls in the parish of Holy Trinity, St. Pancras. Many ladies were involved in the work of many parishes; yet there was always a demand for more. Abraham Hume of Liverpool was not alone when he pleaded for more help from "ladies by courtesy in all our great towns, who have no ties of children or parents or brothers, or kindred of any kind to impede them in the exercise of Christian love."[84]

What was the district visitor intended to accomplish? She did not have the natural access to the poor which manner and accent afforded the lowly scripture reader, and which was seen as valuable in making contact between parson and poor parishioners. Rather she was intended as an agent of reconciliation, providing evidence for the sympathy of God's rich for God's poor. In expressing this sympathy she must herself beware of the same sort of insensitivity against which gentlemen-parsons had to guard. She must learn to treat the poor with respect, to "let them see," as one visitor wrote in the *Guardian,*

> that we do regard them as fellow-beings, as having the same feelings, the same sources of joy and sorrow as ourselves, and the same right to a share of the enjoyments as well as the necessaries of life.

Having developed an easy communication with the poor family, she was expected to distribute tracts, encourage parents to have their children baptized, and read aloud from the bible and Prayer Book when this seemed appropriate. She would maintain a careful register of the families in her district as well as a journal of her visits. These she would review with the district pastor, who could then follow up her work with his professional attentions.[85]

Like scripture readers, district visitors were commissioned to assist the pastor with the spiritual care of the members of his flock. But, unlike scripture readers, lady visitors had other duties as well, for they were directly concerned with the physical and moral welfare of their lowly fellow Christians. In some cases they distributed alms. It was certainly their duty to inform the poor of parochial institutions available to enhance their secular well-being, including schools and dispensaries, libraries and saving schemes. The ladies were expected to bring the possibility of emigration before those who might benefit from uncrowded colonial life, and they were to promote personal cleanliness and proper ventilation. Whenever they could they were to find employment for those who were out of work. Certainly they were to promote the cause of established morality, to "make it thoroughly understood that the church . . . can give no countenance to the idle, drunken or profligate."[86] Such facets of the district visitor's modest auxiliary pastoral role reflected an important this-worldly side of the sacred vocation of the parish priest, a secular dimension of the pastoral profession itself.

IV

The Secular Dimension

BEFORE VICTORIA's reign a good deal of the country parson's life consisted of secular activity appropriate to an educated gentleman who was identified with the landed ruling class. This was particularly evident in the work of clergy as justices of the peace. In pre-Victorian times about one quarter of all county magistrates in England and Wales were clegymen. Indeed, despite developing opposition both from Dissenters and from within the church itself, clergymen continued to accept appointments to the bench throughout the second and third quarters of the century.[1] There were honorable reasons for doing so. On 31 October 1855 a clerical justice wrote in the *Guardian* that, as a magistrate, he could "often . . . effect an amicable adjustment of quarrels among neighbours, and of differences between man and man without 'taking to the law,'" that he could "aid the poor man materially as an ex officio guardian," and that "it is the habit and wish of clerical magistrates as a body to soften the unnecessary rigour of the law." Was it not fairer, he asked, that a clergyman should judge disputes between farmers rather than that one farmer try the case of his "brother"? Furthermore, the precise secular duties of the magistracy were professionally useful to the pastor himself. They forced him into the world of his fellow men and prevented him from retreating too far from the lives and concerns of those whose souls were committed to his charge.

Such arguments as these, however, were losing ground among the clergy. The professional ideal of separate and sacred clerical character discouraged the sort of immersion in secular disputes demanded of a magistrate. It came to be considered improper for a pastor to act as a judge for the Crown, to mediate both the forgiveness of God and the punishment of the state. Moreover, if the clergy continued to accept appointment to the bench it would delay the regular commissioning of "unprejudiced paid officers," magistrates who would rescue local justice from the whims and ignorance of amateurs, whether clerical or lay. The idea that service as a magistrate was an obligation which all competent gentlemen, including ordained gentlemen, were bound to undertake if asked, was thought by Harry Jones to be both absurd and a threat to the professional performance of a priest's pastoral duties. "At this rate," wrote Jones

> he might be doctor, lawyer, schoolmaster, engineer, or anything else demanding the best intellect in the place. He might be so repeatedly split-up and divided that at last the priestly residue became too thin and weak for use.[2]

The increasing reluctance of many clergymen to become magistrates did not mean that Victorian parsons were less concerned about the secular welfare of their neighborhoods (or of the country generally) than were their predecessors. In fact they developed local schools and institutions as never before, and they often took to the public arena to defend their church against encroachment by the state or attack by Dissenters, as well as to campaign for improvement in the moral and material life of the people. Much new style secular involvement was based on the idea that pastors were servants of their people, men who possessed what one writer called "a sort of general commission to promote the good of those among whom they are settled."[3] The priest's "general commission" involved him in a huge variety of trivial secular services. On 12 January 1857 the *Times* remarked sympathetically that a parson was expected to attend to all the "naughty chidren, the weak stomachs, the asthmas, the rheumatisms, and the bad legs of the parish." Edward Spooner observed that the pastor was often the "only known public character" in a city parish, so that he might be required to sign "hosts of certificates of identity for pensioners, for depositors of money in savings' banks, in sick-clubs, etc." Such documents could be signed either by a clergyman or a magistrate. But in urban areas, where few men knew the whereabouts of magistrates, most of this work fell on the shoulders of the clergy.[4] To discharge his secular responsibilities, large and small, as well as to respond effectively to his spiritual calling, the urban incumbent often became an administrator. The *Guardian* called him the "nucleus" of an organization of schoolmasters, teachers, and district visitors; around him "the voluntary energies of the citizens may be gathered and organised for purposes of good."[5]

Pastoral theologians justified the complex and substantial secular dimension of the clergyman's sacred vocation by setting it in a professional context and by giving it professional purpose. Frequently the purpose alleged was quite as secular as the work itself: clergymen were to concern themselves with temporal affairs in order to maintain and promote social and political stability in the parish and the nation. More often than not, however, handbook writers and pastoral commentators cited religious purposes for the clergyman's worldly professional activities. These purposes were of three main types: first, to prepare the way for the Gospel; second, to facilitate Christian reconciliation between individuals and social classes; third, to express the theological conviction that any work for the physical, intellectual, and moral betterment of human beings was itself holy and an essential part of the sacred ministry.

The union of church and state was often viewed as a means of protecting society from political subversion, of preserving law and order, and of encouraging moral discipline in the populace. The clerical magistrate was a symbol of this union as well as an agent of this policy. After 1830 pastoral theologians increasingly discouraged clergy from accepting commisions of the peace, but they were far from rejecting a positive clerical role in the maintenance of political stability. For example R. W. Evans, in his *Bishopric of Souls* (1842), pointed out that watchful clergy pursuing their ordinary pastoral rounds, concerning themselves sympathetically with the needs of their people, were, in fact, a form of preventive police. In the course of his regular visits the pastor would warn publicans and their patrons against illegal and subversive activities. In continual contact with the constable, the clergyman "will be the mainspring of the police of his parish, but like the mainspring of a watch, it [*sic*] would not be seen." Evans's view was shared by pastoral writers and correspondents in the church press throughout the middle decades of the century. In 1853 Alfred Gatty told the clergy that it was their duty to sympathize with workers afflicted by low wages and unemployment and to raise funds for their relief; but he went on to insist that their chief obligation in industrial disputes was to show courage and leadership in order to "expose and overthrow" any political agitators who might attempt to foment disturbance.[6]

Criminal disorder, like political agitation, could be prevented by careful pastoral work. J. H. Blunt thought the clergy were "the most effective national police that exists,"[7] and a writer in the *Guardian* on 1 August 1860 suggested that an increased number of active curates would save the public purse much money currently spent on jails and policemen. This miracle was to be effected, not by asking the curate to act as a government or police spy (as Evans seemed to suggest in the case of political subversion), but by encouraging him to instill a code of respectable behavior among the poorest classes, an ethic which would discourage the development of criminal character. When it became widespread among the "residuum" this new morality would substitute

> habits of obedience for reckless waywardness of will, honesty of principle for the low cunning of selfish and unenlightened impulse, decency and even amenity of manners for the rudeness and coarseness and shamelessness of ignorance.[8]

There were thoughtful and active clergy who found it impossible always to bolster currently accepted values and to advocate economic and political orthodoxy, even in the cause of social and political stability. Some activists rejected the philosophy of the free market as it applied to factory labor; others objected to the working of the new poor law. At least one pastoral theologian, Edward Monro, was convinced that the clergy's sympathy should generally be with wage earners in industrial disputes, that is with those who challenged the status quo and the strict dictates of political economy. Samuel Earnshaw, a Sheffield curate, condemned the use of religion to justify keeping the poor at a static low position in society. A speaker at the Alcester Clerical Meeting on 11 May 1848 expressed some unusually radical thoughts about the revolutions sweeping Europe in that year. The notion that a clergyman was an agent of the state, a substitute policeman, a promoter of "contentment, confidence and goodwill" among the poor, and an evangelist for the doctrine that the working class should be content with its lot was not agreeable to Christian Socialists, nor to some radical Anglo-Catholic clergy in the sixties and afterwards who rejected the idea of an established church altogether. Nevertheless, despite individuals and groups with views of these kinds, a good many clergy (including many pastoral theologians) continued to find the maintenance of law and order a compelling reason for involvement in the secular life of their parishes.[9]

Pastoral writers frequently justified the clergy's secular professional activities on evangelistic grounds: by caring for their peoples' bodies and minds pastors might increase the attractive power of the Gospel. Samuel Best was convinced that people would be far more likely to listen to a clergyman's "spiritual exhortations" after he had proved his concern for their "temporal good." It was unreasonable to expect the poor to develop mature religious consciousness when their conditions of life and work permitted no reflection. James Pycroft thought it perfectly natural that on Sunday the working man was in bed and not in church, for it was his only day of rest. Furthermore "foul airs" and "ardent spirits," both rife in the slums, acted on the brains of the urban poor "like a narcotic." To win the souls of such people the clergyman must first work to change the secular circumstances of their lives, to humanize them before attempting to Christianize them as the London Curates' Clerical Club put it in 1856. Bad housing, overwork, Sunday work, drunkenness, and ignorance were thought of as stumbling blocks to the acceptance of the Gospel by the poor. Clergy participated in public campaigns and national crusades devoted to the removal of the social causes of religious insensitivity. They also provided local clubs, institutions, and schools to offset what one writer called "social hindrances to the spread of Christianity."[10]

Many writers considered it a pastoral duty to foster harmony among their people, both between individuals and between social classes. In the New Testament the reconciliation between man and God effected by Christ has a this-worldly dimension; the church is described as a community of reconciled persons in which barriers and hostilities among human beings are overcome. In St. Paul's view Jews and Gentiles are "fellow citizens," made one by the death and resurrection of Christ who "has broken down the dividing wall of hostility." In the church of the New Testament the aim of reconciliation applied to all human divisions, including that between slaves and free men and that between men and women.[11] For obvious reasons St. Paul did not include modern social classes in his list. Nevertheless, class was the most evident and most conflict-prone form of social division in nineteenth-century England, and it is hardly surprising that clergymen who were familiar with the epistles of the New Testament, and who were ordained to encourage "quietness, peace and love" among their parishioners,[12] should consider it their duty to act as agents of reconciliation between classes as well as between inividuals in their neighborhoods.

Bishop Wilberforce thought "the gentlest and most discerning touch" was required for this work. Difficult and delicate as was the task of bringing together estranged individuals, that of overcoming antipathy between class groups was even more so. There were duties and occasions which could serve that end. Charitable giving might "arouse feelings of sympathy with the poor," and church sponsored recreational organizations and events afforded "meeting points" between the classes.[13] However, more than this sort of thing might well be required. It might be necessary for the clergyman to speak out against customs which worked injuries on neglected or excluded groups.[14] Churchmen sometimes found it difficult to unite the need for prophetic outspokenness with the imperative of reconciliation. Sometimes the combination was impossible. For example, when Edward Girdlestone campaigned to improve the miserable condition of agricultural workers at Halberton in the 1860s he certainly earned the hatred of local farmers. On 10 April 1867 the *Guardian* wrote that Girdlestone had abandoned his true pastoral function as reconciler, that his proper role was not to be a class champion but to be a social conciliator, smoothing the differences between laborers and farmers. This the *Guardian* simple-mindedly thought Girdlestone could have achieved by encouraging the laborer to increase his skill "so that his labour would be worth more than it is now," and at the same time preaching greater liberality to the farmers.[15]

However facile and unheroic, the *Guardian's* stand reflected an ideal of reconciliation within a relatively static social structure which was surely held sincerely by many thoughtful and well-meaning mid-Victorian clergymen. When Samuel Wilberforce insisted that the clergy should be "reconcilers of those inevitable differences which divide classes," he undoubtedly took the word "inevitable" seriously. St. Paul believed that the reconciliation of slave and free man in Christ could be achieved despite the continuation of slavery; so Wilberforce believed that class reconciliation could be effected without fundamental change in the structure of Victorian society. He, along with many others much interested in strengthening the parish ministry, thought that the clergyman's proper social aim was to reduce conflict and to strengthen the bonds between inevitably unequal classes.[16]

There is evidence that this object was achieved occasionally, partially, and incidentally. For example Brian Harrison has shown that such moral reform causes as the temperance movement and the Lord's day observance crusade (in which clergy played important roles) did unite elements of the working classes with their betters, thus "blurring class distinctions."[17] For the most part, however, class reconciliation was an object for which the Victorian church and clergy were ill-fitted. It was surely fanciful for Edward Monro to imagine that the church might become a "peace-maker between the two contending parties of our great commercial society" when the mass of the working class felt no identification with the church at all.[18] How effective an agent of reconciliation was a church whose pastors felt it necessary to provide separate services for different sorts of working men, separate forms of family prayer for poor and rich, which could not accommodate itself to a working-class priesthood, and in which those poor people who did come to ordinary services sat separately from the better-off elements in the congregation? How useful a machinery for reconciliation was an urban parish structure the units of which reflected the increasingly monochrome class aspect of city and suburban neighborhoods?[19]

Some pastoral theologians questioned the traditional division between sacred and secular spheres of pastoral activity. In their view the professional servants of a God who was "born in the likeness of men" (Philippians 2:7) could not accept any sharp distinction between the salvation of souls and the healthy development of minds and bodies. Furthermore, priests of Christ's church were obliged to concern themselves as much with the social relationships between men and their neighbors as with the religious relationship between men and God. Deep awareness of the

70

social implications of incarnational theology was especially evident among liberal and broad churchmen. In his handbook *Priest and Parish* (1866) Harry Jones went out of his way to stress the clergyman's responsibility to undertake good works which those with a narrower view of religion might think to be outside his vocation. In Jones's opinion it was the pastor's duty to interest himself in such things as "the drainage of the fen," "the building of the cottage," "the digging of the parish well," "extortion in the village shop," and "bad economy in the cooking of the peasant's food." This he does

> distinctly as a priest on divine grounds. He does not try to make his spiritual instruction more palatable by mixing it with material good things. His concern for their bodies is not a concession to the lower appetites of the people. He makes temporal good witness to them of a God of order, justice, health, economy, reproduction, purity and power. He shows them the Divine Presence of that Will which set man to have dominion over the earth and thus leads their ideas of holiness beyond the round of Sabbath-keeping, bible-reading and family prayer. He makes them feel the encircling contact of the Kingdom of Heaven in those matters which we naturally degrade to the level of mere worldly business. Thus he connects the worship of the Sunday with the work of the week.[20]

As well as justification for the priest's secular work, the pastoral theologians offered precise advice about how that work should be done.

One area of clerical duty about which they found it particularly difficult to provide clear advice was the distribution of alms. Traditionally Christians had recognized an obligation to help their poorer brethren, and charity had been understood as the simple act of giving by the rich to relieve the distress of the poor. By the 1830s, however, this obligation had been a good deal modified by contemporary economic and social theory. It was generally believed (and the belief was enshrined in the new poor law) that poverty among the able-bodied was the result of fecklessness and improvidence rather than misfortune. Reform, not relief, was therefore required. Handouts, whether in the official form of outdoor relief or the unofficial guise of charitable gifts to individuals, too often discouraged the qualities of character necessary for the development of independence and productive citizenship.

There is abundant evidence that this attitude dominated the thinking of many pastoral writers in the decades between 1830 and 1870. Writing in 1839, Samuel Best warned his readers that "indiscriminate almsgiving" was "charitable anarchy," wasteful of money and demeaning to the receiver. It fed poverty and resulted in the perpetuation of pauperism, itself fundamentally the product of wickedness. Harry Jones felt clergymen must recognize that even "though the sufferer himself be innocent, yet if we could analyse every case of destitution, we should find its cause in disobedience to some law, that is, in sin."[21]

Despite the vogue of self-help theory and the development of state machinery for dealing with paupers, Victorian pastoral theologians found it impossible to reverse Christian tradition completely and recommend the abolition of charitable handouts altogether. Although they generally agreed with W. W. Champneys that "the regular systematic relief of the poor" was a government responsibility to which parishioners contributed in their rates, they recognized that respectable parishioners should be spared the humiliation of official pauperism in times of severe temporary distress. W. H. Lyttelton, for example, in 1852 listed five particular purposes for which he felt a clergyman might legitimately provide charitable aid to needy parishioners: (i) for living expenses during prolonged illness, especially when the expenses were not covered by a friendly society or provident club; (ii) for domestic help in late pregnancy and after childbirth, especially in cases of mothers with large families; (iii) for the provision of nutritious food to convalescents who were weak but just able to work and therefore ineligible for aid from a friendly society or club; (iv) to old people without children to care for them, and whose former employers were neglecting them; (v) for occasional assistance to the parents of very large families. Aid for these purposes might be dispensed either in the form of cash or tickets (which could be exchanged for goods at the shops of cooperating tradesmen); on the other hand it could take the form of clothing, or, indeed, of food. The "soup kitchen" was not uncommon. Robert Gregory discovered that some of his poor parishioners at St. Mary's, Lambeth, actually had died of starvation during winter and early spring. With the help of an outside benefactor he established a soup kitchen at which about five hundred quarts a day were dispensed during the worst of the winter, a total of sixteen thousand quarts during a full season. In fact recipients of Gregory's soup paid a penny for each quart, an amount that covered about one third of the cost.[22]

Despite the general unpopularity of the handout as a way to deal with poverty, some churchmen believed that carefully controlled parochial charity could play a positive though indirect role in pastoral work. On 24 February 1869 the *Guardian* pointed out that giving and receiving alms could well be genuine expressions of "the mutual relations between fellow Christians united by neighbourhood"; thus charity could serve to strengthen the sense of local Christian community, of commitment to a common cause. In 1869 the Charity Organisation Society was founded. Harry Jones found the Society very useful in preventing the abuse of handouts by crafty indigents. According to Jones the rigorous sifting of the motives of the poor by the C. O. S. "peeled the skin off much plausible imposture and helped many would-be donors to give money with wholesome effect."[23]

In dealing with poverty the Victorian clergy had much greater faith in self-help than in handouts. The list of parochial clubs, associations, and projects founded to increase the material comfort, strengthen the health, and ensure the security of parishioners was long indeed. Many of them were described by pastoral writers intent on improving the professional performance of the clergy generally.[24] Throughout the period, for example, there are numerous references to lying-in charities and baby-linen societies to accommodate mothers and very young children; typically Samuel Best insisted that only mothers who themselves showed "some corresponding degree of providence" should be permitted to benefit from the latter. Best went on to describe a School Coal and Rice Fund at which parents whose children were regular attendants at school got "premiums" to buy coal and rice at reduced rates. In London Robert Liddell wrote in 1853 of a self-help project to aid distressed needlewomen. In the next decade Robert Gregory's parochial society for unemployed needlewomen in St. Mary's, Lambeth, managed to bid successfully for large government contracts and to make hundreds of such women self-supporting. In rural areas no self-help project was more popular than the provision of allotments, small plots of arable land, often parts of the glebe, let at reduced rates for cultivation by poor parishioners. John Sandford thought that allotments gave poor men a stake in the existing social and political order, a "sense of property." The system was conceived both as a remedy for the evils of unemployment and as a means of moral improvement. "Drunkards have been reclaimed," wrote Sandford, "sabbath breakers brought to church, and a general reformation effected by means of it." Furthermore the food produced helped to keep the cultivator and his family off the rates.[25]

Two types of self-help institutions deserve more extended consideration, not only because they were common, but especially because they required considerable administrative capacity in the clergymen who promoted them. First were those institutions and clubs which encouraged the poor to save in order to meet recurring unavoidable expenses and the emergencies of unemployment, illness, old age, and death. Second were those which provided medical care for poor and working-class parishioners on a contributory basis.

Whereas middle-class and relatively prosperous working-class parishioners could afford to put aside regular amounts in a savings bank, no such means were available to suit the circumstances of the really poor. Regular trustee savings banks normally demanded a minimum deposit of one shilling, far too much for the very poor. Furthermore the procedures for withdrawal and deposit at such banks were complicated and their hours of opening were often inconvenient for the poor.[26] Early in the century a number of clergy attempted to provide savings facilities for their parishioners by acting as agents for district savings banks. H. C. Ridley, for example, wrote in 1829 of collecting pennies, sums far less than the banks would accept individually; he conveyed the accumulated pennies to the bank for deposit. Other clergy received, and themselves retained, the pennies of the poor for safekeeping. T. J. Rowsell, for example, brought together about £250 of the savings of his poor Stepney parishioners in 1850; by 1857 the sum had risen to £1,750, even though Rowsell offered no interest at all on these deposits.[27]

By the 1860s a good many penny banks had been established to encourage regular saving among the very poor. In his *Directorium Pastorale* (1864) J. H. Blunt provided detailed information about the procedure for setting up and continuing such banks as parish institutions. He thought that interest might be guaranteed by the subscriptions of affluent parishioners. In small parishes, where the mechanism was not complex, he advised combining it with a clothing and coal club so that some of the savings of the people could be repaid (at their option) in fuel and fabric bought in bulk at favorable rates. Blunt referred his readers to a pamphlet by J. Erskine Clarke, vicar of St. Michael's, Derby, who, in 1859, was secretary of the Derby Workingmen's Association Penny Bank. This was not a parochial institution, and of the twenty-six penny banks Clarke knew to exist in England in 1859, only one seems to have been officially church related. Many in towns were attached to workingmen's associations and mechanics' institutes.[28]

Parish provident societies, unlike most penny banks, directed savings to particular ends. Sometimes the subscriptions of parishioners were collected and set by to pay for recurring expenses such as rent, fuel, and clothing. Other parochial provident funds had broader aims. Samuel Best had a comprehensive society in his parish of Abbott's Ann during the 1830s and 1840s to provide "for sickness and old age, for the settlement and advancement of the subscriber in life, or for such other purposes as conduce to his permanent comfort." He wrote, in 1849, that two-thirds of the parish population participated in this fund. In 1845 John Sandford's parish of Dunchurch supported three distinct provident funds: for adults, widows, and schoolchildren respectively.[29]

The purposes of a parochial provident society such as that at Abbott's Ann were not unlike the practical aims of friendly societies founded and operated by working men themselves, although they lacked the traditional pub nights and yearly celebrations, social functions of the friendly societies with which clergy often found fault. In fact, some clergymen showed considerable interest in friendly societies proper as agencies for alleviating the hardships and reducing the insecurities of working-class life. Furthermore, as a speaker told the Oxford Clerical Association in 1859, the investment of friendly society funds in savings banks and government securities contributed indirectly to peace and good order. Members of such societies developed an interest in the maintenance of political and economic stability and would themselves be indisposed to join in disturbances.[30]

One handbook writer, the anonymous author of *The Parish and the Priest* (1858), was himself drawn into the life of a local friendly society in an unusual way and to an extraordinary degree. For years the local society in his neighborhood had followed the usual practice of meeting monthly in public houses; contact with the parson had been confined to the annual anniversary service and sermon in church. On one particularly riotous annual feast the police were called, a fight followed, and several members were jailed. Following this event a number of angry wives approached the parish priest for his advice, assuring him that "they would make their husbands do anything that he advised." "I had been standing at the foot of the tree with my mouth open for a long while," he wrote, "but the apple popped in at last." The parson's influence, combined with that of the working-class wives, brought about a remarkable reform of the society. Meetings were transferred from pub to infant school, and the annual club feast was transformed into an affair of cake, tea, and dancing. The priest himself became secretary of the friendly society, and in his handbook he advised the clergy to take any opportunity to follow his example. He cautioned his clerical reader

> to act as secretary only; to be ready with advice . . . if it is asked for, but not to volunteer it . . . [for] any attempt to interfere or to intrude upon the independence of the club would be resented, and very properly.[31]

Ever since New Testament times the church has been involved in healing the sick. Rooted in the doctrine of the Incarnation and in the healing activities of Jesus himself, this involvement has taken many different forms in the ages between the crucifixion and Victoria's reign. The classic English pastoral theologians of the seventeenth century, George Herbert, Richard Baxter, and Gilbert Burnet, all recommended that clergymen and members of their families act as medical attendants in the absence of dependable professional practitioners.[32] During the eighteenth century the English clergy visited the sick as part of their religious duty, and many of them made substantial contributions to the establishment and maintenance of hospitals. The medical profession remained unorganized and divided throughout that century. The science of healing was unsophisticated and the professional quality of English medical training remained low until well after 1800. Clergymen could still master a useful number of the available healing arts, and they were often in positions to provide medical care when a qualified doctor was unavailable.[33] In his *Parochial Duties* (1829) H. C. Ridley wrote of the clergyman's responsibility to prescribe medicines, and in the remoter parts of the country the personal practice of curative medicine by parish priests evidently continued for some time. By the middle of the century, however, this amateur activity was declining, at least in urban areas, in the face of the increasing sophistication of medical science and the unification and professionalization of medical practice. Indeed pastoral theologians of the sixties advised clergy not to treat their people medically. Instead of administering medicine they should know the "terms of admission to the nearest hospital" and be prepared to provide transportation thereto for their ailing parishioners.[34]

Withdrawal of the parson from the front line of medical care did not mean that he lost interest in the health of his parishioners, nor that he merely shuffled them off to the nearest hospitals. Some Victorian clergy took an active part in the provision of nursing care for the sick poor.[35] Many supported the cause of sanitary reform and public health. Others, surrounded by poor parishioners who could not afford private doctors but who shunned the humiliation of reliance on the poor law, organized parish dispensaries and administered local contributory health insurance schemes.

In his *Parochialia* (1845) John Sandford recommended the plan of his own "Medical Union" which had been functioning for several years in the country parish of Dunchurch. The purposes of his scheme were two: to provide security to "the sober and industrious members of the working class" of his parish in times of sickness, and to ensure prompt payment to local medical practitioners who often had difficulty collecting bills from the poor. Sandford's scheme was by no means self-supporting. The annual premiums of two shillings six pence for each adult member of the union paid about half the costs, and the remainder was covered by donations. A similar plan, adapted to the circumstances of urban life, was established in the parishes of SS. Paul and Barnabas, Knightsbridge, in 1849. Yet another scheme, described in detail by the author of *The Parish and the Priest* (1858), involved five medical attendants and included over two hundred members. In that case the pastor maintained a "depot for drugs" at the parsonage. He himself obtained drugs at wholesale prices and he translated the Latin in which doctors' prescriptions were written. Although not engaged in any significant degree of personal medical practice, that particular parish priest provided both the initiative and the organizational skills to establish a considerable health care scheme, and he continued to supervise the whole plan including the dispensary.[36]

As the "sanitary principle" took hold of early Victorian England many of the clergy became increasingly involved in public health, in preventive rather than curative medicine. For Charles Kingsley the sanitary cause became a public mission, but there were other clergy, less prominent on the national scene than Kingsley, who also worked hard for the improvement of housing and sanitary conditions. William Cadman of St. George's, Southwark, for example, exhibited the same enthusiasm and gift for ordered work in the realm of public health that he showed in his more strictly spiritual tasks. Over a period of three or four years he pressed the local board of works to undertake sanitary improvement in a sensible and organized way. "The first thing," he recalled, "was to get the lighting, then the paving, and then the water laid in the courts which five years ago were scarcely visitable." Harry Jones, another London slum priest, considered the improvement of public health to be an important pastoral obligation. He warned his St. Luke's, Berwick Street, parishioners away from a polluted well by hanging a placard on it with the inscription "Dead Men's Broth." Jones worked with a doctor in "a hand to hand fight" with the cholera for six weeks in 1866, identifying cases and burning clothes. At that time he called a meeting of cooperating tradesmen and shopkeepers to divide

> the parish into districts which they visited two and two together, like apostles . . . of the kingdom of health, which is God's. They poked into every drain, ashpit and water-tank. . . . I had provided them with . . . printed instructions which they showed to the tenants of the houses, bringing about such a scouring . . . as had never been seen before. . . . The premises were cleaned, traps mended, tanks emptied and the proper supply of water was seen to.[37]

Physical health, material welfare, and economic security were not the only secular aspects of parishioners' lives which interested the parish clergy professionally. Indeed more time and thought (and money too) were invested by the clergy in their peoples' intellectual development and in the increase and improvement of their leisure time than in all the other sorts of charities, institutions, projects, and campaigns that they undertook.

Mid-Victorian clergymen took a great interest in the recreational opportunities and habits of their poor parishioners. Although some clergy sought extra holidays for workingmen, simply in order to deprive them of an excuse for neglecting worship on Sundays, many others wished to see the time available for recreation increased on health grounds. In 1858 J. Erskine Clarke expressed anxiety about the "millions of our toiling men and women so urgently driven by the high pressure of the labour market." Ten years later George Huntington traced the increase of "fatal heart complaints" to the pressure of constant attention to a single duty. "We resemble high-pressure steam engines," he wrote, "always working at full power"; he thought that the "safety-valve of repose" was needed "to let off the steam of our overwrought energies." W. H. Lyttelton advocated half-holidays, early closing, and the development of a rich selection of leisure occupations for the people in order to improve their mental health and to enrich their culture. He feared that the life of the manual worker was "in danger of becoming . . . a long heavy sleep broken only by fever-dreams of wild excitement and intoxication." Whereas he believed that "utilitarians" wished "to turn this great world which God made so full of manifold and various life into one enormous kitchen garden," Lyttelton wanted to develop some recreational "flower gardens," and to make sure the poor were given time for their cultivation.[38]

Many clergy felt an obligation to change the way that the poor used the free time they already possessed, an aim in which they had the support of significant elements among the respectable working class itself.[39] Pastors opposed drunkenness and sexual vice, and they tried to deprive taverns of their centrality in the recreation patterns of laboring men. One focus of this effort was the campaign to reclaim annual feasts to respectability; another was the movement to replace yearly statute hirings by employment registration centers and modest nonalcoholic entertainments. Pastoral theologians wrote a good deal about alcoholic dissipation and licentious dancing at the fairs, and about the alleged profiteering of pub keepers. They thought reform rather than suppression was the proper solution to these problems. Such reform must involve both a radical change of fair customs and a change in fair management, from the pub keeper and the people themselves to local gentry and clergy. One new pattern acceptable to the clergy was to transform the fair into a church-centered harvest festival, followed by an enormous (but highly respectable) village party. J. H. Blunt wrote about one such party that consisted of a meal of beef, mutton, plum pudding, and tea. Psalm-singing and healthy games followed, and the whole ended with a "vigorous dance round the sheaf" and the singing of God Save the Queen. Clerical writers thought that such reform of local feasts would not only produce improved morality and sobriety among the people, but also effect a reconciliation among parishioners of different social classes, and so recover "those times when our country was known, not as the land of gloom and care and money-getting, but as 'Merry England.'"[40] Obviously this sort of transformation would have altered the traditional feast beyond recognition, and, one suspects, would have destroyed its attractiveness as a genuine recreational event of the rural poor. In fact traditional fairs did decline during the last half of the nineteenth century, but chiefly for reasons other than the opposition of the clergy and gentry.[41]

The pastoral writers disapproved of a great many traditional working-class pastimes besides drinking and fairs. Prize fights, dog fights, cock fights, and ratting matches were condemned outright. Music, dancing, and the theater were considered unacceptable in the forms presented by music halls, dancing saloons, and "penny gaffes"; but they were thought capable of redemption. The evils associated with the theater were "drunkenness and licentiousness, the doubtful morality of plays [and] the unworthy character of the majority of the actors." These could be expunged, thought Erskine Clarke, and the intrinsic value of theatrical performances retained, if a local "committee of supervision" were to censor every performance. With adequate oversight by respectable persons, dancing too could be reclaimed and then reformed to provide "the maximum of disciplined exercise with the minimum of familiarity."[42]

Clergymen's doubts about dancing and the theater contrasted with their unrestrained approval of musical concerts, choral festivals, and instrumental lessons. Outdoor sports were also selectively recommended for the poor, and the parish clergy were encouraged to develop clubs and contests among their parishioners. J. W. Burgon was especially keen on local cricket clubs. He found it

> hard to believe that young men so drawn together for purposes of amusement by their clergyman, and finding him the liberal patron of their sport, would be disinclined to listen to him when he asks so slight a favour as that they would no longer prove obstructive on Sunday.[43]

Many clerical writers sought to include the workingman's wife and children in his recreational pattern, and to make his family life an important part of his leisure activity. "It is not fair," wrote George Huntington, "for the husband to leave his wife to bear her cares alone, that he might indulge systematically in amusements." Clergy were encouraged to develop counterattractions to pub and dancing hall which would include her as well. Playing fields and public parks, free public libraries, railway excursions (under suitable patronage and control), and public concerts (not on Sundays) would provide places and occasions for family recreation which could be enjoyed by children and both parents together. Money saved by shunning pubs would be used by the virtuous father to improve the quality of home life:

> There would come a better house where flowers would be able to bloom. . . . Soon might follow, if not the piano, . . . at least the violin, or the accordion, or the musical glasses; and then the recreation of the tired husband would be in the sweet society of his wife and children.[44]

Desirable as home-centered recreations certainly were, they were not enough. Young men who had left school and their parents' home, but had not yet married and settled down, were a major pastoral problem. Furthermore, many homes were themselves thoroughly undesirable, overcrowded, dirty, and noisy. Even if a laborer's home were attractive, and he himself had developed a model family life, still he needed "a little healthful excitement" now and then, a place outside his home "which shall correspond to the clubs of the wealthier sections of society."[45] During the 1850s and 1860s many laborers' clubs, institutes, and workingmen's associations were begun in both rural and urban parishes, founded by clergymen and backed financially by their affluent parishioners. In many respects they constituted a network parallel to the mechanics' institutes, many of which were also under strong clerical patronage by the middle of the century.[46] Church clubs or institutes for workingmen were by no means directed by their working-class members. Robert Gregory attempted to allow full self-government to a Lambeth club, but he reported that the experiment resulted in squabbles, schisms, and failure. It is impossible to judge whether this failure arose from managerial incompetence, from an unsuitable constitution which excluded traditional working-class recreations, or simply from working-class suspicion of church and clergy. In any case it was an unusual experiment. Normally such clubs were controlled by the parish priest, assisted by a committee of workingmen and a few better off honorary members.[47]

The church workingmen's club or institute was generally well-equipped to provide rational recreation. It usually had a reading room, stocked with a few newspapers, books, and periodicals, together with such games as chess and checkers. It might also possess a smoking room, and field teams for cricket and other outdoor sports. Popular lectures, readings, and musical events normally formed parts of the club program. Coffee and tea were available at paticular times, and in a few places (according to the *Guardian* on 10 March 1858) a "limited quantity of beer" was dispensed. Erskine Clarke described a number of successful clubs of this sort. He was especially impressed by the Lichfield Association which had between one hundred and two hundred members, and by a Dover "Youth Institution" at which, in 1859, 150 young men "were gathered, instructed and amused."[48]

Clergymen thought of the workingmen's club as an antidote to vice, a counterattraction to the pub, and a point of contact between the pastor and his working-class parishioners. It was also an important element in the growing provision for adult education at the parish level in mid-Victorian England. Indeed the line between the clergyman's view of rational recreation and his idea of adult education was exceedingly hard to draw. Books and other reading materials in the club rooms of church workingmen's institutes were thought of both as opportunities for recreation and as means of self-improvement. Here and there clergymen were active in setting up "village reading rooms" for a wider public. Encouraged by pastoral theologians (who provided lists of suitable books) clergymen established parish libraries in which they provided alternative literature to that found in pubs and sold by door-to-door salesmen throughout the country.[49]

The clergy heartily disliked most of the popular literature available to the ex-pupils of their parochial schools outside such controlled libraries and reading rooms. Especially they detested that sold by the ubiquitous travelling book hawkers. According to the author of *The Parish and the Priest* (1858) these tradesmen placed a few respectable items at the top of their packs; but underneath were not merely coarse and ribald works, but

> well-written, clever . . . compositions of the foulest and most corrupting nature possible, calculated to sap the very foundations of the peoples' morals and religion and to teach them sensuality and profligacy of which they have never until lately dreamed.

Clergy were advised to keep an eye on such men, as well as on neighborhood shops and to "beg or bribe them, at least not to sell the poisonous police and highway literature to our boys and girls."[50]

In fact churchmen went into competition with the common hawkers. In 1859 the Church of England Book Hawking Union was founded, the fruit of an experiment begun in Hampshire in 1851, which gradually spread through many counties. Its object was to meet with popular but respectable literature the "appetite for reading created by our multiplied schools." Christian hawkers were employed to act as agents working under the patronage of parish priests and of the local gentry. By 1860 seventy church book hawkers were employed under the direction of fifty-seven local associations; in that year approximately twelve thousand books were sold mostly to farm laborers. In 1861 there were sixty-two local associations and eighty hawkers who visited throughout their allotted districts at intervals of from one month to a year. Modest growth seems to have continued for a few years, although in 1864 the number of church hawkers was reduced to thirty-six.[51]

A controversy developed among the clerical supporters of the Union concerning whether or not hawkers should concentrate wholly on selling religious books. Erskine Clarke and others who were especially concerned to improve working-class recreational patterns advocated that "books of good honest humour," "useful books of history and biography," and even chess and draughts should be sold by the hawkers. But others objected. One clerical gentleman thought that even the most respectable secular reading could be subversive when put in the hands of the lower classes. He had heard, he said

> of an instance where some boys at a reformatory school, who, after reading the history of Guy Fawkes, were debating whether they should go and set fire to the Reformatory or the stacks on the farm. Ultimately they chose the farm, and the result of their reading was the destruction of the stacks.[52]

Although the Book Hawking Union had declined by the late sixties, similar schemes continued to function at the local level. For example in one Leeds parish an association of young people was established especially to sell "periodicals of a sound and religious character" in the places where the members worked. In 1867 this parochial association sold more than fifteen thousand publications.[53]

One type of direct contact between the parson and the poor was afforded by popular lectures, delivered from time to time by the clergyman to a club or adult group in his parish. These talks had both recreational and educational purposes and were usually on secular, frequently practical, subjects. As lecturer, the clergyman functioned not as a religious leader but in his traditional role as the learned man of the community. J. W. Burgon suggested "the nature of the Atlantic cable" and "the electric telegraph" as appropriate topics. W. W. Champneys recommended biographical, historical, or scientific subjects, although he especially favored practical ideas on improving the quality of life. "It may be shown to a poor man," he wrote in *Parish Work* (1866) "that clean windows and white walls are medicine, and that a little time and a few pence spent on these may save a doctor's bill and help to keep off sickness." However Champneys was quite prepared to use lectures for propaganda purposes as well. For example he recommended a "salted lecture" on "the life of Mohamet, as giving an account of one of the great standing impostures of the world." In Champneys's experience the clergyman met people at lectures that he would never encounter in church, and whom he might introduce to the Gospel later on.[54]

From early in the century parish priests had formed regular adult classes in the autumn and winter, partly to allow illiterate or barely literate adults to acquire the rudiments of learning, and partly to give further instruction to boys who had left the parochial schools at the age of ten or twelve. Not all adult classes were confined to reading, writing, and arithmetic. Nor was additional instruction always in religion. At St. Mary's, Lambeth, for example, Robert Gregory organized a "School for Drawing and Modelling" to accommodate members of the labor aristocracy who were past the need for elementary instruction; founded in the 1850s, this special evening school had 150 pupils in 1863 and over two hundred by 1866. Whatever the curriculum, evening schools formed part of many clergymen's strategy to maintain contact with rebellious youth, and as such had a disciplinary and moral purpose beyond their function as agencies of adult education. They provided a constructive evening occupation for "those who would [otherwise] be loitering about," whose contact with the religious life of the church was broken, if, indeed, it had ever existed.[55]

The clergy themselves evidently did most of the teaching in these adult schools, a task that normally occupied them on two or three days a week for two hours each evening. All too often the pastor's devotion to teaching was not matched by pedagogical competence. Communicating simple knowledge to simple people was not easy for university educated clergy, and failure to do so was one factor among several that led to the collapse of a considerable number of evening schools. Nevertheless there is plenty of evidence that many adult schools succeeded and that, although the total number of pupils under instruction was modest enough, it was increasing. In the decade from 1847 to 1857 the scholars in church evening schools in England and Wales increased from 22,550 (.13 percent of the population) to 54,150 (.27 percent of the population); by 1867 there were more than four thousand such schools, with nearly 150,000 scholars.[56]

Older girls and women were taught in separate evening classes, often specializing in sewing and homemaking, subjects thought to be appropriate to their sex and role in life.[57] W. W. Champneys recommended "Mothers' Meetings" to his fellow clergy, gatherings which he himself had successfully organized in his London parish of St. Pancras. At these meetings the wives of workingmen were trained in the basic elements of household economy, to make and mend their husbands' and children's clothing, and to manage family finances. Just as he "salted" his lectures to workingmen, so Champneys injected direct religious teaching and explicit evangelistic purpose into his mothers' meetings. Along with the classes in practical work went Bible lessons, and Champneys hoped to get at the adult men of the parish indirectly through their wives. "The truly Christian wife," he wrote, "who has herself been brought to a lively faith and living obedience *since* her marriage, will be cheered by the hope that she may save her husband." This scheme evidently worked at St. Pancras. Through the influence of their wives a class of over fifty workingmen came regularly to study the Bible with Champneys himself.[58]

Sunday schools continued to grow through the first three-quarters of the nineteenth century, and handbook writers considered their development and supervision to be important parts of the clergyman's vocation. Early in the century (as also late in the eighteenth century) Sunday schools dispensed a considerable part of such secular knowledge and sacred learning as was available to the children of the poor. When large numbers of elementary day schools were opened in the first half of the nineteenth century, Sunday schools concentrated increasingly on religious knowledge. After it became difficult to give the traditional emphasis to denominational religious instruction in government-supported day schools under the revised code of 1861, some clergymen argued that the work of Sunday schools was more vital than ever.[59] Pastoral theologians warned their readers against poor parents who exploited church Sunday schools for baby-sitting purposes. "Tommy and Polly are packed off between nine and ten o'clock," wrote Harry Jones, "[where] they are safe till one. The parson minds them; the church is a consecrated nursery." Sometimes parents excused their own delinquency at public worship by referring to their children's attendance at Sunday school.[60]

Many clergy provided weekday infant schools or nurseries for children up to the age of six, partly to remove them from the "evil influences" of their homes and to aid mothers who must go out to work, but chiefly to drill them in "habits of regularity, tidiness and general obedience" and so prepare them for the work of the regular parish day schools.[61] On those elementary day schools, at which children from the ages of six to twelve received basic instruction, most clergymen concentrated their most vigorous educational efforts in the half century before the Education Act of 1870.

By the 1860s it was becoming clear to many people (including some churchmen) that the church's considerable efforts to provide elementary education were inadequate to the enormous challenge of industrial England: the schools built were too few, the teaching provided was too skimpy, and the church base was too narrow to meet the demands of Victorian society. Indeed the whole denominational system of English elementary education, even when supported by government grants, was not enough. The Education Act of 1870, which provided for rate-supported state schools, marked the beginning of a decline in the dominant role of religious bodies in primary education. Before that happened, however, the Church of England had lavished her resources freely on her parochial day schools, acting often (but not always) through the National Society. At first on their own, and after 1833 in partnership with government, churchmen had managed to provide over 19,500 such schools by the 1860s. In them some learning was given to about one and a half million children, over seventy-five percent of all the children who attended any schools in England and Wales. Between 1811 and 1870 over fifteen million pounds were privately given and subscribed (over and above the government grants) for the construction and maintenance of Church of England parochial schools.[62]

The burden of planning, financing, and managing these thousands of schools rested on the shoulders of the parish clergy. It was usually the parish priest who first saw the need for a school, who then set about raising money for site and building, and who often contributed the largest sum himself. On the success of his local effort hinged the grants from the National Society and the government which frequently were essential to make the project possible.

Handbook writers complained about the deep involvement of the clergy in begging for money, and their complaints were echoed by practising pastors, especially in urban districts. On 6 January

1857, for example, Abraham Hume of Liverpool wrote to the *Times* that for eight years he had been completely responsible for the survival of his parish schools:

> Every farthing necessary for their support during that time has been raised by my own personal canvas. . . . During the past year I have made many hundreds of calls, and spent more time on this business than on all my parochial and pastoral visitation, though I am quite unable to see why a clergyman should be expected . . . to be perpetually responsible for duties which belong to all citizens in common.

One day Hume walked seven miles, called at fifty-four places of business, and went home with only four subscriptions totalling three pounds. This sort of frustrating and exhausting activity encouraged an unhealthy clergy-centeredness, thought the author of *The Duty of a Layman in the Church of England* (1856), while also making it very difficult for the parson to find time to fulfill his pastoral duties. Associated in the minds of his parishioners with appeals for money, he was "shunned like the tax gatherer," and so lost his effectiveness as their moral and spiritual guide. Worst of all, because he took unaided responsibility for building and maintaining schools, they were seen as his alone; "the laity are shut out, or shut themselves out" from work which should have been theirs to share.[63]

In fact there are examples of clergy in urban areas who succeeded in gaining substantial middle class lay support, and who even attracted the participation, cooperation, and resources of local workingmen in establishing schools. Hook managed this in Leeds, and in the early fifties nearly four thousand poor members of William Ackworth's parish of Plumstead donated £339 for new schools. The same sort of thing happened during the same years in a suburban slum area near the Victoria Docks where the vicar of Plaistow, R. W. B. Marsh, and Antonio Brady, a senior civil servant, worked hard to establish schools. Marsh and his wife set out to solicit donations from the local inhabitants. According to Brady, as they passed the houses of the poor "the people run out and say 'do not pass my door: I should like to give something.'" About one-tenth of the population of four thousand poor parishioners were contributors to the schools, giving sums varying from a farthing to two shillings and sixpence. "Our object," said Brady, "was to give them an interest in the work."[64]

Such an interest was usually difficult to arouse, and the pastoral theologians could find little hope for much increased giving by laymen for church schools. Like Walter Hook before him, Harry Jones concluded that only the state could cope with the huge problem of financing elementary education. It was a view shared, among others, by Abraham Hume who, by 1869, was convinced that only a full system of state financing could guarantee proper schools in poor districts. Certainly this development would greatly benefit parochial clergymen. Removal of the huge fund-raising responsibility from their shoulders would mean, wrote Hume, that "the lives of the local clergy would be prolonged, if not in some cases actually spared."[65]

Just as they took the leading role in planning and financing parochial schools, so the parish clergy normally controlled the life and teaching in those schools. In 1839, the year the Committee of Council was established to supervise government grants for elementary education, most parochial schools in union with the National Society were "under the exclusive superintendence of the clergy."[66] This clerical dominance continued in church schools despite attempts by the Committee of Council in 1846 and afterwards to undermine it by insisting on lay management committees for schools assisted by government grants. The militant high churchman G. A. Denison believed that absolute clerical control of parochial schools was a guarantee of orthodox teaching as well as evidence of the union of sacred and secular learning and of the church's exclusive right to educate the nation's children. A good many pastoral theologians, not themselves afflicted by the sacerdotal rigidity and explosive temperament characteristic of Denison, agreed with him about the central role of the parish priest in the management of parish schools. Edward Monro, for example, wrote in 1850 that "the parish priest [must] be the actual manager and teacher of his school . . . the master but his temporary *locum tenens*." His view was shared by both J. J. Blunt and J. H. Blunt. Harry Jones advised incumbents always to appoint the teachers in their parochial schools, personally to conduct all correspondence with the government education office, to regulate the school fees, and to arrange and preside at all school committee meetings.

They should also supervise the teachers and develop the curriculum. Furthermore the clergyman himself was expected to undertake at least some of the religious instruction in the parish school, to conduct school prayers and special services of worship, and to examine the children on their knowledge of the church catechism.[67]

In order to teach effectively himself and wisely to supervise subordinate teachers, the clergyman was advised to devote some attention to methods of instruction and to the ways and habits of children. Edward Monro was especially insistent that the clergyman-teacher be sensitive to the uniqueness of each child, and that he adjust his teaching to meet the needs of individuals. J. J. Blunt and John Sandford were keen that clergy actually develop good pedagogical technique. Writing in 1861, Sandford warned pastors that

> teaching is a science; it does not come by intuition. And in days when so many schools have trained masters . . . it is more than ever necessary that the clergy, with a view to their own usefulness, should be "apt to teach." It is therefore well that a practical acquaintance with the system pursued in our training colleges should be pressed upon candidates for Holy Orders as an essential branch of education.[68]

The massive clerical effort to provide England with schools for the poor was undertaken for reasons as various and from motives as mixed as those that lay behind the whole secular dimension of Victorian pastoral work. Recent social and educational historians have tended to emphasize secular motives for the church's enterprise in elementary schooling.[69] The maintenance of social stability and the extension of moral respectability were unquestionably prominent considerations in the minds of clerical school builders and managers. There is no need to search between the lines for such secular motives in the writings of the pastoral theologians. John Sandford thought that the children of the poor "cannot too early learn that . . . they must avoid giving any trouble or disturbance to others, and that by neatness, order and arrangement this may be avoided." Samuel Best expected the children to acquire the "subordination of discipline"; J. J. Blunt wanted them to gain an "instinct for order"; and Harry Jones hoped they would catch the "contagion of obedience." Under the clergyman's influence, wrote J. H. Blunt, the children of the poor may "become morally and religiously fitted to do their duty in that state of life to which it shall please God to call them."[70] Desirable moral qualities were to be included within the secular instruction of the school. Thus punctuality, honesty, and thrift could be taught in the context of arithmetic lessons. Girls must be instructed in sewing and knitting; along with these technical skills, they may also learn how much better off they will be to engage in such work at home rather than to take to factory or farm labor. The poor girl must be warned against any attempt to grasp at independence, and taught instead "that her true economy . . . is to husband her partner's earnings, rather than attempt to augment them by her own."[71]

Despite this sort of evidence it would be a mistake to think of the clergyman's secular motives for educating the poor as entirely repressive. Writing in 1849, Samuel Best expressed a hope that church elementary schools might provide an avenue for poor children to rise in social and economic status, a means by which the "barriers of poverty are broken down." There are examples of parsons with simple humane motives for instructing the poor, men who sought to improve their parishioners' quality of life. W. H. Lyttelton, for example, in his schools at Hagley introduced children to physiology, sanitary science, and local geology, as well as carpentry, gardening, gymnastics, and drilling. "With regard to education," he said, "our aim should be to cultivate human nature as a whole in all its powers—bodily, mental and spiritual."[72]

Although they never attempted to hide what they considered to be the secular values of church schools, pastoral theologians always considered church education to be a religious enterprise. No doubt it is well to be cautious about accepting religious rhetoric and to be sensitive to latent secular purposes lurking beneath the declared religious aims of parish schooling for the poor. It is equally important, however, not to discount the religious motives of religious men, and to remember that pastoral concerns were naturally central to the pastoral profession.[73]

The declared primary purpose of the clergyman's personal activity in his schools, and the root aim of the whole enterprise, was religious: to prepare the children for heaven. "Education," wrote Samuel Best, "is the commencement on earth of a system which is to carry us forward into heaven." However mundane the educational ambitions of parents for their offspring, the priest's chief hope was to save the children's souls. Most clergy certainly valued their pupils' intellectual accomplishments, but they valued moral and spiritual improvement much more. No doubt many were like E. J. R. Hughes, a Yorkshire incumbent who taught writing and arithmetic to children "in order that he might for the last half hour impress them with religious truth."[74]

The school also had indirect pastoral purposes. It was seen as an instrument of parish evangelism, a means by which the parish priest might reach the adult poor. Through the children a pastor could learn about their families, knowledge which would help him immensely in his ministrations and in his efforts to build up a Christian community in the parish.[75] Even if this hope of using the school to develop the adult church failed (as the evidence shows it usually did) still the clergyman hoped that the school would be "the nursery of the church," or "the germ of the coming parish." He hoped that one day the children upon whom he was lavishing such care would become a strong working-class congregation. Moreover his duties within the school gave him opportunities to think and express himself simply and extemporaneously, skills of great value in preaching to the adult poor.[76]

One reason why pastoral theologians emphasized the religious motivation for the secular activity of parish work was entirely professional. They feared that too much worldly work, undertaken simply for social and humanitarian reasons, would erode the clergyman's distinctive professional character. Samuel Wilberforce, for example, worried lest pastors should lose sight of their sacred calling in enthusiasm for promoting "general decency and amendment . . . in society"; the great Evangelical, Daniel Wilson, feared that worldly business too often diverted them from their proper "ministerial and spiritual duties."[77] Such clergy as Wilberforce and Wilson, men who developed the Victorian ideal of the professional pastor, were determined that the parish priest's secular activity, however substantial and varied, should remain but a dimension of his sacred vocation.

V

The Making of a Clergyman

Victorian pastoral theologians believed that effort and training were necessary for a man to develop clerical character and pastoral proficiency. Some tensions certainly existed between the traditional understanding of ordained ministry as a divine vocation and the growing conviction that it was also a profession requiring special knowledge and skills and a particular style of life. A professional man could be "made," his character formed by fellow humans, his mind informed with special knowledge and trained in necessary techniques and skills. On the other hand a "call" was heard, not manufactured; it was normally recognized in particular qualities of personality and in natural abilities which could be developed but not actually created.[1]

One evidence of such a call was the possession of what Edward Monro called pastoral "genius." The possessor of this gift

> will go into a cottage, and with saying *very little*, not "reading the bible aloud," *doing* scarcely anything, not giving a *penny*, will come out having done a work and effected a result, which other men who have not that power, with an hour's hard work at the same cottage, reading half an Epistle

through, lending tracts in large print fresh from the Christian Knowledge Society, talking, arguing, reasoning, and giving half-a-crown to boot, will not effect.[2]

Purity of motive was another indicator of true vocation. A number of pastoral theologians warned their readers against unworthy "second motives," namely, seeking a leisured literary life, "indulgent recreation," financial security, preferment, or social advantage through ordination.[3]

The authors of occupational guide books for parents seeking careers for their sons stressed the professional rather than the vocational aspects of the sacred ministry. These writers thought their readers more interested in decent wordly prospects than in a heavenly summons. H. Byerly Thomson, for example, devoted a chapter in his book *The Choice of a Profession* (1857) to a review of "the Church as a Profession." In it he quickly put to one side the "delicate question of original motive," the matter of "a sacred calling," and went on to observe that in the ministry "there is as much desire for increased emolument, reputation, and advancement, as in any other calling." After discussing the structure, educational requirements, and patronage system of the Establishment, he listed what he conceived to be the practical advantages of the clerical profession: "opportunities for early independence"; "comparative security of position"; "opportunity of leisure"; "absence of any risk of total failure"; "easy work compared to the struggles of other callings"; "ready admission into society"; and (the closest he came to anything like vocational idealism) a "satisfactory sphere of usefulness." In view of the worry about clerical poverty and poor income distribution so common among churchmen in the fifties and sixties, it is curious that Thomson considered the financial reward of the clergy to be better than that of many other professional men, including barristers.[4]

The vocational idealism of the pastoral theologians contrasted strikingly with the careerism of such as Thomson. Realists among the committed clergy and laity occupied a middle ground. For example, Edward Bartrum, a clergyman who campaigned to substitute merit for private interest in making clerical appointments and promotions, warned candidates for ordination against feeling guilty or becoming discouraged just because they had felt no special "call." He believed that a just and regular system of appointment and promotion would attract many honest, earnest, and useful men who might never hear a heavenly summons, but who could be assets to the church. Conybeare thought such men (neither motivated by "heroic self-sacrifice" nor secular ambition, but who sought "a routine of kindly and useful, if not laborious service, with a respectable position in society") already constituted the largest single block of clergy a decade before Bartrum wrote.[5]

Whatever the differences about motivation, idealists and realists among mid-Victorian clergy were united in a common conviction that the pastoral profession needed recruits whose characters were properly formed and who possessed the special knowledge and skills required to function effectively as parish priests. The preface to the ordinal in the Book of Common Prayer demanded that candidates for the diaconate and the priesthood should be "tried" and "examined" (as well as "called") before being admitted to those offices. Interest in the preparation of men for parish ministry was uncommon in the eighteenth century; but it was not absent, as is evident from the lives and opinions of Gilbert Burnet and Thomas Wilson.[6] The mid-Victorian clergy shortage caused some to emphasize the need to regularize and multiply the means for preparing men to be pastors. However neither Prayer Book tradition nor worry about recruitment wholly accounts for the intense concern about clergy training in the middle years of the nineteenth century.

In the first years of the century the Church of England clergyman was undergoing an important professional reorientation which affected the doctor and the lawyer as well, and which had profound implications for professional training generally. Rather than being a man whose professional title was defined principally in terms of his status as a gentleman, the priest was becoming a person with a distinct occupational role requiring particular knowledge, special skills, and a recognizably professional quality of life. In the old hierarchical society of late eighteenth-century rural England the typical incumbent was a gentleman with a village church at his disposal, the ordained and established teacher of the community whose pulpit was the principal platform for disseminating local information.[7] It was that status which qualified him as a magistrate and as the manager of local charities, which rendered him a natural crony of the gentry, and which justified the expectation that he would possess a degree from

Oxford or Cambridge, the sign that he was a gentleman with intellectual interests. The degree requirement testified to no significant amount of theological knowledge and to no pastoral training whatever, lacks which few churchmen in the eighteenth century thought of as defects. The particular tasks which attached to ordained status (liturgical, homiletical, and pastoral) were thought to require no special formal training and their performance was amateur rather than professional.

The belief that a clergyman should be an educated gentleman persisted throughout the nineteenth century and was defended by a good many pastoral theologians for years after the conditions that justified the belief had passed away.[8] By the middle of the nineteenth century the average Englishman was as likely to be a townsman as a villager. Although the typical Church of England parish remained rural, most professional interest concentrated on the cities, where the gentleman-parson was a fish out of water. In suburbs and in the countryside the incumbent was unlikely to be *the* learned man whose words were accepted by all except a few sharp Dissenters and agitators. Many of his hearers were probably as well (or better) educated than himself, perfectly capable of ordering the secular affairs of the parish, and very unlikely to accept unsupported theological assertion from the pulpit. "One kind of faith is gone," said Sir John Pearson at the church congress of 1867,

> the faith that comes without inquiry . . . handed down from one generation to another, and assented to as a tradition not to be disputed. . . . Faith is now the result of inquiry and conviction and does not come by nurture and habit and association only. . . . The clergy have ceased to be what they once were, the educated class. They cannot guide the laity as they will. They cannot dictate to them what they are to believe. . . . Inquiry once aroused must be answered now, not by the *ipse dixit* of the priest, but by reason and argument.

Facing these new style congregations caused anxiety to some clergy who not only doubted their capacity to cope with theological problems and doubts, but were insecure about their general secular knowledge as well. One agitated parish priest wrote in 1866 that he felt quite overwhelmed when he mounted the pulpit to see "hardheaded, brain-working men" before him.[9]

As the rising level of congregational education placed new demands on the preacher for theological competence, so also the growing complexity of society and the increase of specialist knowledge in many fields threatened the amateurism of much clerical activity. Many roles traditionally performed by clergymen were being assumed by other professional men. Medical skills became more scientific, and as trained medical men became generally more available most of the paramedical functions of the pastor disappeared; in 1866, Harry Jones wrote that in the sickroom only "the administration of conventional religious consolations" was left to the clergyman. Likewise the spread of popular literature and journalism undercut the role of the preacher as the principal communicator of information and ideas. Teachers, sanitary engineers, and civil servants of many sorts all narrowed the scope for traditional clerical ministrations. It was a change that Harry Jones, for one, did not regret. Whereas in a remote colony a priest might have to do many things "little belonging to his vocation," Jones thought that such activity was unnecessary and undesirable in a "settled civilised country."[10]

Devoted members of the established church in that "settled civilised country" did require of their clergy sound theological and general knowledge, hard systematic work, and the skills necessary to evangelize and provide pastoral care for the teeming masses of a mobile urban society. The clergy were not expected to withdraw wholly from secular affairs, but it was assumed that their worldly occupations would normally be capable of theological or pastoral justification, and that they should not attempt to compete with other recognized professional men. Most of those who demanded a professionally competent clergy, especially if they had been affected by the Evangelical or Oxford movements, insisted that such competence include personal holiness.

Such new style clergymen needed to be trained. Pastoral theologians thought that the scanty provision for professional training in the early Victorian church was a disgraceful aspect of the generally scandalous eighteenth-century inheritance. Criticism on this score was well-advanced by the time Victoria came to the throne. It continued through the 1850s, reached a crescendo in the 1860s, and continued long after 1870. It was voiced by men of many shades of churchmanship, including some who used the need to develop adequate professional training as a lever to defend or to reform the ancient universities and cathedrals. Recognition of the need was a bond among men who could not agree on the methods by which it was to be met, who often distrusted each other's churchmanship, and who fought among themselves about many ecclesiastical matters.[11]

Comment on the inadequate provision for clergy training focussed on three particular deficiencies, well-expressed by the secretary of a clerical meeting at Alcester on 4 October 1863: (i) "absence of accurate theological knowledge"; (ii) "want of a complete acquaintance with the technical duties of the pastoral office"; and (iii) "neglect of all specific moral or spiritual training for the ministry."[12] The emphasis given to one or other of these varied to some extent according to churchmanship. Anglo-Catholics and high churchmen particularly stressed the desirability of "specific moral or spiritual training," the formation of clerical character, although they also insisted that the clergy should have a thorough grounding in the received theological tradition. Evangelicals, although certainly conscious of the value of a distinct clerical style of life, took special interest in practical pastoral and homiletical training. Broad churchmen, keen to commend the faith to modern intellectuals, stressed critical theological learning and broad general scholarship.

Liberals and broad churchmen thought that the best places for an ordinand to acquire general learning were the ancient universities. After 1860, when critical biblical and historical scholarship really impinged on the English scene, they also felt that the great universities alone (certainly Cambridge; the Oxford of Pusey and Liddon was doubtful) could generate independent critical theology appropriate to the age of agnosticism.[13] Early in the century the state of theology at the ancient universities was feeble indeed. A very small part of the work for a regular degree, divinity was not taught systematically or seriously, and no special classes were required for ordinands, although many Evangelicals had the advantage of informal instruction from Charles Simeon and his successors at Cambridge. Voluntary lectures were offered by divinity professors for graduates who wished to remain at Oxford or Cambridge while awaiting the minimum age for ordination to the diaconate. The situation improved slowly between 1830 and 1860.

A successful "voluntary examination" in theology was instituted at Cambridge in 1843 which most bishops required graduates of that university to pass before ordination. A similar examination at Oxford, established a year earlier, failed for want of episcopal support. Notwithstanding the Cambridge examination, and despite the appointment of more numerous and more conscientious divinity professors at both universities (of whom J. J. Blunt of Cambridge was particularly well-known), theology was not a regular degree subject at either place until the 1870s. Even then the highly prescriptive notion of "accurate theological knowledge" held by Pusey, Liddon, and Burgon at Oxford differed remarkably from the critical scholarship of Hort, Westcott, and Lightfoot at Cambridge (where F. D. Maurice was given a professorial chair in 1866). Whereas the Cambridge theology curriculum was the work of critical theologians, the honors school of theology at Oxford was thoroughly conservative, a final effort to retain an island of dogmatic churchmanship in an institution rapidly losing its old character as an Anglican clerical enclave.[14]

Despite the curious revival of Oxford theological conservatism in the late 1860s, most high church and Anglo-Catholic pastoral theologians were dubious about the adequacy or security of the ancient universities as centers of orthodox theological teaching. Instead they looked to diocesan theological colleges where graduates could be indoctrinated while acquiring the stamp of true clerical character. On the other hand Evangelicals were reluctant to abandon hope that the old universities might be made to supply appropriate courses in theology.[15] Two new church institutions, Durham University and King's College, London, did provide professional instruction in divinity for ordinands. In 1833 Durham developed a licentiate in theology, open both to graduates and nongraduates. A theological department was added at King's in 1846 which offered a two-year course in theology and pastoral training. Both these institutions inspired favorable comment from clerical writers and both developed into useful sources of nongraduate ordinands. Neither became an important alternative to the ancient English universities as a source of clergymen in the mid-Victorian church.[16]

Many a conscientious ordinand spent the months between university graduation and ordination in solitary preparation for his bishop's examination. Handbooks of pastoral theology often contained lists of books which the authors thought appropriate for this time of private study. Even if undertaken diligently by able men, independent work of this sort simply added specialized intellectual preparation to the general academic background provided by Oxford or Cambridge. The uncertain demands of the bishop's examination, and the young graduate's natural temptation to relax intellectually after taking his degree, reduced the value of this period of unsupervised study. Ashton Oxenden felt that his own year of solitary preparation had been a "poor prelude to that consecrated life to which I was soon to be called." In Oxenden's view a far better way to spend the year or so between graduation and the minimum age for ordination was to serve "a kind of ministerial apprenticeship" under the direction of a competent and experienced parish clergyman. "Theological reading will do much," he wrote

> but . . . if we have never knelt by a sickbed; if we have never taken a class in a Sunday School; if we have never come into actual contact with the wants, and habits, and ways of the poor; how can we be fitted for so great a work as the spiritual management of a parish.[17]

Practical parish training of this kind was the most popular remedy for the second great defect in the professional preparation of the clergy, "want of a complete acquaintance with the technical duties of the pastoral office." Pastoral writers frequently compared supervised parish training for ordinands to the clinical training demanded of medical students or the articling required of law students. An efficient instrument for guaranteeing professional competence, this sort of "apprenticeship" also provided an admirable opportunity for a young man to test his vocation and so reduce the chance of being trapped by ordination into a mistaken and irreversible calling. It was a form of training that required careful direction by competent practicing parish priests. Oxenden thought that "each bishop should have a list of a certain number of experienced, active, earnest, devout ministers" whom he knew to be capable of directing and encouraging ordinands in this way. Like Walter Hook, Oxenden looked forward to the day when six months of supervised pastoral training of this sort would be required of every candidate for ordination.[18]

Although it was never made compulsory, a good many graduate ordinands in the Victorian church did receive this sort of practical instruction for a period of from three to twelve months. Probably the best-known Victorian trainer of clergy in this style was C. J. Vaughan, whose numerous "doves" at Doncaster and the Temple included some famous men. Between 1861 and 1875 Vaughan supervised over two hundred graduates of Oxford and Cambridge, teaching them how to manage a parish and its schools, how to visit the sick, and how to prepare sermons. He also advised his pupils on their theological reading and assisted each of them to select a diocese and to find a curacy. Edward Girdlestone did similar work at Deane in Lancashire; so did John Sandford in Dunchurch and a number of other parish priests in different parts of the country.[19] Their purpose was to provide ordinands with a distinct part of their professional training, the practical part. If (as was certainly the case) ordinands also read some theology in the interstices of parish life, and if the immersion in pastoral routine gave them opportunities to appreciate and absorb the distinct qualities of clerical character, these were considered valuable by-products of an essentially practical training.

Advocates of parish training for graduate ordinands embraced many types of churchmanship. Among them were Walter Hook, a high churchman, and the ritualist Bryan King. However Anglo-Catholics and high churchmen were more likely to recommend that the graduate should enter the disciplined community life of a theological school or seminary under the authority of a diocesan bishop and, if possible, be attached to a cathedral. Although some advocates of such graduate colleges (Samuel Wilberforce among them) assumed that practical pastoral training would be included in the curriculum, this was not generally so. Anglo-Catholics like H. E. Manning, Philip Freeman (third principal of the Chichester college), and H. P. Liddon (vice-principal of Cuddesdon, 1854-59) either excluded practical training altogether or else assigned it a low priority in their discussions of the purposes of theological colleges.[20] In his scheme of pastoral instruction Liddon gave a minor place to what he called "the external duties of the Christian priest." In his view the primary need in professional training for the ministry was not practical instruction in sermon composition, or visiting, or administering schools; rather it was to show the ordinand how to develop his "inward life," to cultivate moral

101

sensitivity and personal piety, to mold his character and discipline himself so that he might learn to *be* a priest. Although in 1868 Liddon insisted that "the first function of a theological college is to teach theology," in his opinion it was not the main purpose of such teaching to impart knowledge, much less to raise problems of criticism or speculation. Rather, academic theological study was undertaken that the ordinand might build an intellectual base for the priestly life. The purpose of theological teaching in a professional school or seminary was to indoctrinate men called to a holy vocation, to inculcate what Philip Freeman called a theological "way of viewing men and things." In fact the real focus of Anglo-Catholic college life was neither academic study nor practical training; it was moral and spiritual growth, fostered by disciplined community life, a regular round of offices, sacraments, and meditation under the close personal supervision of the principal and his assistants. These things formed the essence of the ideal Anglo-Catholic seminary.[21]

This was a conception of professional theological education which contrasted remarkably with that prescribed by the proponents of supervised pastoral training. Instead of plunging him into the practice of parish ministry in the real world of town or village, the collegiate ideal required that the graduate ordinand be removed from the scenes of ordinary secular life into an isolated community where distinct clerical character could be formed in a disciplined society and where dogmatic truth could be imparted and absorbed without distraction. Advocates of this system were particularly anxious that the secularity and moral temptation of university life be left behind during these months of preparation for ordination. "In an institution for training clergy," wrote Manning in 1846, "all the sanctions and associations must be ecclesiastical; every object should be emblematic not of the academy but of the altar, not of scholars but of apostles." As Oxford and Cambridge came to look less and less like Christian institutions, some champions of theological colleges (including Liddon) thought that they might develop into full-fledged church universities.[22]

Although many of the founders of the first colleges for graduate ordinands did not share the full Tractarian opinions of Manning, Freeman, or Liddon, yet in the popular mind those views became associated with the idea of diocesan theological colleges. The

102

association certainly had some basis in fact: Manning was an important figure in the founding of the colleges at both Chichester and Wells; Charles Marriott, one of the original Tractarians, was the first principal of Chichester; and Freeman, a principal theorist of the Anglo-Catholic view, was Chichester's third principal. Liddon, the most eloquent exponent of Anglo-Catholic ideas on clerical training, was vice-principal of Cuddesdon and the dominant influence there from 1854 to 1859. Suspicion of extreme churchmanship was one factor that inhibited the general acceptance of diocesan theological colleges. There were other problems as well. The low priority such colleges gave to supervised parish training was one; another was "mutual jealousy," allegedly generated between ordinands and ordinary laymen when the former were removed from normal society; yet another was the additional expense of a postgraduate year in college. However, the main reason why relatively few graduates went on from Oxford and Cambridge to diocesan theological colleges was probably the lack of worldly advantage in doing so. In 1865 Philip Freeman (by then Archdeacon of Exeter) noted that the colleges were languishing for lack of graduate pupils. The reason, he thought, was simple:

> It is that in England everything has its market value, and the time of the young men and the money of their parents, unless there be a fair prospect of advancement in the position of life which they choose, are not likely to be expended on theological studies.

Only the bishops could change this situation. If they made it clear that a man's chances of preferment would be enhanced, and his opportunity for promotion improved, by a postgraduate year at a theological college, then, said Freeman, "I believe that you would ... find no difficulty in inducing persons to enter these colleges."[23]

Advocates of parish "apprenticeship," and of diocesan theological colleges such as Chichester, Wells, and Cuddesdon, assumed that the principal problem in theological training was the professional formation of graduate ordinands. Indeed many of those who wanted to widen the social range of recruits to the ministry sought to retain the graduate standard by creating ways for poor men to earn degrees at Oxford and Cambridge.[24] By the middle of the century, however, it was becoming clear that the

103

training of university men was only part of the problem. Year by year the numbers of nongraduate literates ordained increased. Some private theological colleges (several of them founded before 1830, others established under Evangelical auspices after 1845) were especially planned for these nongraduates. Up to the end of the 1860s the largest colleges of this type were St. Bees (founded in 1816) and St. Aidan's (founded in 1846), both Evangelical institutions which provided two-year courses of study. Two new universities, Durham and King's, and Queen's College in Birmingham, deliberately tailored their training in theology to accommodate men without previous university experience. Even though bishops were sometimes ready to ordain nongraduates with no formal training at all, men who had been "individually fitted for the work," nevertheless some colleges for literates and the course leading to associate status at King's (the AKC) did come to occupy a significant place in professional training.[25]

St. Aidan's, Birkenhead, was a particularly interesting Victorian foundation for training nongraduates. Its founder was Joseph Baylee, a combative Irish Evangelical who was well-known for his defense of the literal inerrancy of scripture and for his pugnacious anti-Romanism. At St. Aidan's he combined collegiate community life, a traditional course of lectures and readings in theology, and a remarkable program of supervised pastoral training which foreshadowed much modern theory concerning the way a pastor should learn the skills of his vocation.

The academic curriculum (composed of biblical studies, Latin, Greek, and Hebrew, church history, and readings in Hooker, Paley, and Butler) reflected Baylee's desire to have his college accepted by bishops and others who continued to insist that clergy should have the education of gentlemen. Unfortunately, those who came to St. Aidan's were unprepared for such an academic diet. In 1867 a memorial presented to the college council by about one-quarter of the student body contained the complaint that

> men are admitted who (having absolutely no knowledge whatever of Classics; but very little of their English grammar; and in fact knowing absolutely nothing but their Bibles) find themselves suddenly plunged into the very midst of advanced studies in Theology and Classics.

Faced with inadequately prepared students Baylee responded by lowering standards and resorting to teaching methods which were resented by his better pupils. This breakdown of the academic side of college work was an important factor leading to Baylee's resignation in 1868.[26]

Baylee had always claimed that the main aim of his institution was to provide pastoral training, not theological learning. For this purpose he considered it a great advantage for a theological college to be near the challenges and opportunities of a large town. St. Aidan's itself orginated in the Parochial Assistant Association, formed by Baylee and a considerable group of local clergy in 1846 to provide lay visitors for the parishes of Birkenhead and Liverpool. In fact the "parochial assistants" were the students of the new theological college, and the project had twin aims from its beginning: to evangelize the urban masses of Liverpool, and to train mature nongraduates for the ministry. Students in the college were required to visit in urban parishes for three hours on three days a week under the supervision of the local incumbent. Contradicting the view that academic theological learning and active pastoral training should be kept separate, he insisted that the field work at St. Aidan's

> instead of being a hindrance . . . is a very great help when a young man is reading the theory of religion in his books. Then, when he is going from house to house with these questions brought out into practical everyday life, it makes him understand the books much better, and he . . . sees the application of them.

Every student was assigned a street or two of houses. He visited the families in those streets regularly and reported weekly both to the local clergyman (who had previously prescribed the limits of the student's pastoral activities, whether prayer, reading, delivering cottage lectures, or distributing tracts) and to Baylee himself. "Every Saturday morning," said Baylee in 1857,

> they bring me a printed return filled up, showing what they have been doing. They bring me all the difficult things they have had to deal with and they get from me the most suitable answers to give in such cases.

Sometimes the students were employed to undertake what Baylee called "statistical visitation." Six or eight students would be assigned to a clergyman who wanted an exact description of his parish population, including the religious affiliation of each family. Abraham Hume, the well-known priest-statistician, received just this sort of assistance from St. Aidan's students in his slum district of Vauxhall. The combined program of statistical survey and supervised pastoral visitation was very large, and it evidently continued at least until Baylee left Birkenhead in 1868.[27]

Most of the students trained by Baylee were mature; their average age was in the middle twenties. Most of them came from other trades and occupations, many from posts as clerks in merchants' offices, and some from positions with very high incomes. A good many were former Dissenting ministers, mostly Methodists.[28] Baylee was very sensitive to the charge that he turned out ordinands who were socially below par, and he insisted repeatedly that the majority of his students were gentlemen, and therefore would be suitable incumbents for English parishes. Not everyone agreed. In a series of letters published in the *Guardian* in 1863, Archdeacon John Allen of Shropshire attacked St. Aidan's as a place of "feeble educating power," whose products tended to "degrade the character of the English clergy." In one letter Allen recounted a tale that Dr. Baylee attended a meeting of cab drivers and "told the men 'that if any of them wished to leave their present mode of life, and would like to become clergymen, he would not only receive them at St. Aidan's, but would assist them with money.'" Baylee denied this story. However it is hard to accept his boasts about his students' high social status without qualification. Certainly the record of students admitted just after Baylee left St. Aidan's (the only such list that exists) contains a good many sons of parents far below the mid-Victorian standard of gentility.[29]

Both Baylee's inability to create a theological curriculum suitable to the requirements and the abilities of his clientele, and his nervousness about the social status of his students, demonstrate the power of the gentleman-theory of ministry in the Victorian church. Baylee recognized the need for a nongraduate ministry; he saw the importance of effective pastoral training, and he developed an imaginative means of providing it. Yet even he felt it necessary to justify his students on social as well as professional grounds. The widely held conviction that a proper English clergyman must have a degree from Oxford or Cambridge (or at least from Dublin), and the prejudice against clergymen who were not also gentlemen, severely hampered St. Aidan's, as they also restricted the contribution of all the colleges for literates. Insufficient financial backing, isolation, overdependence on a single man, lack of adequate staff, unreliable support from the bishops, and uncertain acceptance by the church, all kept theological colleges for nongraduates weak and relatively small. Such colleges formed no part of the church's plan of ministry simply because there was no such plan. Nevertheless they managed to provide some professional training for men who were needed in the church's mission to industrial society. Furthermore, as the story of St. Aidan's shows, these colleges are not barren of educational significance for those interested in the techniques of professional training for pastoral ministry.

The making of a Victorian clergyman did not end when he was ordered deacon in his early twenties. Throughout his ministry means were available for what Walsham How described as his "continued education."[30] If he were appointed an assistant curate, his pastoral labors were supervised by a senior priest. Whether or not he had the advantage of such supervision, he was expected to continue reading seriously, and he was quite likely to be caught up in the developing network of clerical associations and gatherings in which pastors learned from each other by means of argument and discussion.

An essential part of pastoral training was a well-ordered curacy, particularly for a deacon without the experience of a parish apprenticeship before ordination. Ashton Oxenden told the Canterbury Convocation in 1858 that at least one year of such post-ordination training should be required of every deacon before he was permitted to undertake the sole charge of a cure of souls. In his *Parish Work* (1866) W. W. Champneys lamented the plight of the professionally ignorant neophyte clergyman who, because he had never worked under supervision, was forced to "learn by experience, costly to others and painful to himself." In 1863, convocation listened to John Sandford review his own case:

> I was dismissed from the schools of the University on the Friday and was ordained on the Sunday week, and then put in sole charge of a parish of between 7,000 and 8,000 souls, to

whom I ministered for two years, till my health was so impaired that I had to leave the charge.[31]

The key to a successful curacy was effective supervision by a conscientious and efficient incumbent. In the view of men as far apart in churchmanship as the Evangelical Daniel Wilson and Bishop James Fraser, such supervision was a very important responsibility of the rector or vicar. It was a responsibility taken very seriously by many distinguished pastors, including Walter Hook in Leeds and the two great Evangelicals, William Cadman and W. W. Champneys. Champneys, for example, regularly met with his curates individually, and once a week he gathered them together for a class in pastoral theology based on their current work. A good supervisor would direct the reading as well as the active work of his curates, encouraging them to develop the habit of regular daily study. Bible reading and classical theology were usually recommended as the staple of such study; most of the handbooks by pastoral theologians received good reviews in the church press, and they were often commended to young parsons as important professional aids.[32]

Sooner or later a clergyman was likely to be sent out on his own, to be assigned his own cure of souls often in the remote countryside or the depths of an urban slum. Without the regular support of fellow curates or a supervising rector he was then expected to keep up his reading and devotion, to maintain a professional style of life, and to cope efficiently with all manner of pastoral problems. In the bad old days of the eighteenth century a young incumbent was likely to plunge into the life of local society unencumbered by that sense of distinctiveness and holiness which inhibited the free social relations of many clergy in Victorian times. For this reason the eighteenth-century clergyman rarely needed to depend on the society of his fellow clergy in other parishes, unless, of course, he were an Evangelical.

From the middle of the eighteenth century Evangelical clergy banded together in clerical societies "to strengthen each other's hands in the work of the Lord."[33] Despised and rejected by the wider church, themselves rejecting the local society of unenlightened squires, they met to encourage each other in worship and Bible study, to raise money for the support of poor Evangelical undergraduates at the universities, and to exchange ideas on the problems and opportunities of parish work. During the nineteenth century Evangelicals continued and expanded this informal system of clerical societies and meetings, some of which became large and famous (that founded by Daniel Wilson at Islington, for example).[34]

In Victoria's reign similar societies were founded by clergymen of very different schools of churchmanship. The ideal of distinctive clerical character was accepted by clergymen of many opinions who began to feel uncomfortable in local secular society, and who therefore looked for the friendship and support of fellow pastors. As professional interest was aroused in the techniques and skills of parish ministry, churchmen of various types formed private associations to discuss these matters, as well as theological topics, among themselves. Such clerical societies remained informal, and membership was often confined to men of similar ecclesiastical views. The record of one high church society which met monthly at Alcester from 1842 was published as *Eighteen Years of a Clerical Meeting*, and contains reports of discussions on a huge range of pastoral and liturgical subjects, as well as matters of general public concern. Another society, also high church in membership, met fortnightly in Oxford in the 1850s and 1860s and included such Anglo-Catholic luminaries as the Tractarian Charles Marriott, R. M. Benson, and H. P. Liddon, as well as two prominent authors of pastoral handbooks, J. H. Blunt and J. W. Burgon. Subjects discussed by the Oxford society ranged from practical problems encountered by local clergy visiting the Radcliffe Infirmary to "Indelibility of Orders" and "the state of the risen body." Although they generally found clerical exclusiveness distasteful, some clergy of broad church views evidently felt the need for a professional gathering of this sort. Harry Jones was the principal founding member of the Curates' Clerical Club in London, originally an association of assistant curates in the West End which began in 1856 and lasted well into the twentieth century. Shortly after its foundation it began to elect some incumbents and other senior clergymen to membership. By the early sixties both A. P. Stanley and F. D. Maurice were members, as well as a number of other liberal-minded clergy including J. Llewelyn Davies, W. H. Fremantle, and Stopford Brooke. Maurice attended the monthly meetings regularly from 1862 until 1866, contributed to the discussions, and entertained the club at his home on the very night of his appointment to a chair at Cambridge in 1866. As with the Alcester and Oxford associations, the CCC (as it was known) discussed many matters, both practical and otherwise; they ranged from subjects such as "district visiting," "night schools," and "how to reach the upper classes," to "the Divorce Bill before Parliament" and "Colenso and the Pentateuch."[35]

The spread of private clerical societies was paralleled by the development of formal structures which also encouraged professional self-consciousness and the articulation of practical pastoral theology in the Victorian church. This formal movement included the revival of ruridecanal chapters and convocation as well as the establishment of diocesan conferences and annual church congresses in which the laity as well as the clergy were represented.

The office of rural dean is an ancient one. Traditionally an agent of the bishop and subject to the authority of the archdeacon, the rural dean was the senior priest in a group of neighboring parishes. Between the Reformation and the early nineteenth century the office had declined in importance in some dioceses and disappeared altogether in others. During the nineteenth century it was revived, and the appointment of a rural dean was often accompanied by the establishment of an official local clergy meeting over which he presided. By 1880 all English dioceses had rural deans and ruridecanal chapters. On 6 January 1861 Bishop Montagu Villiers of Durham wrote in the *Guardian* that he considered the rural dean "a great bond of union between the bishop and his clergy" and a "means of making the whole ecclesiastical machinery of a diocese to work with regularity and comfort to the clergy." Bishops expected the ruridecanal chapters to meet regularly to discuss what Villiers described as "practical subjects." Undoubtedly this often happened, and some clergy certainly preferred this inclusive official form of professional gathering to the private societies. Others, however, were suspicious of what looked to them like an instrument for enlarging the bishop's power, a system of episcopal espionage which they feared would infringe on the traditional independence of the incumbent.[36]

Convocation, an exclusively clerical body, was revived in the early 1850s, largely through the efforts of high churchmen, particularly Samuel Wilberforce and Henry Hoare. Its membership was heavily weighted in favor of the higher clergy: of 146 members in the lower house only 42 were elected by the beneficed parish clergy. Curates were completely unrepresented. Although Ashton Oxenden was a regular participant in important convocation debates, his fellow Evangelicals were generally dubious about this exclusively clerical body which the *Christian Observer* suspected of "sacerdotal pretensions irreconcilable with liberty and truth."[37]

In contrast to convocation, the annual church congresses were open and unofficial. From their beginning in 1861 laymen as well as clergymen contributed to the debates, many of which were on subjects of professional pastoral interest. Once again many Evangelicals were doubtful about what appeared to be a centralizing movement under high church auspices. But to a far greater extent than convocation, the congresses of the 1860s did gain the support and participation of clergy and laymen of all parties. This support was given eventually to diocesan synods and conferences which were revived from the early 1850s and spread very rapidly throughout the church. At these local conferences, as at the church congresses, laymen participated with the clergy, and a great many topics of professional concern were considered.[38]

The Victorian clergyman's morale, his attitude to his work, and his capacity to grow in his vocation were all much affected by the complexities of patronage and promotion in the church. Competence and efficiency played but small roles in determining the pay and promotion of the clergy at a time when merit was increasingly accepted as the proper criterion for advancement in many occupations, when high standards of pastoral merit were being defined in handbooks, and their attainment encouraged by pastoral training.

For the five thousand assistant curates in the mid-Victorian church the possibility of advancement to a decently endowed benefice was chancy indeed. In 1867 there were just over seven thousand livings worth over two hundred pounds a year (a hundred pounds below the widely accepted minimum); for those livings nearly six thousand occupants of poor benefices competed with the five thousand assistant curates and some of the several thousand other clergy not in parish work. Samuel Wilberforce concluded that it was "arithmetically impossible that the existing incumbencies can afford maintenance within a reasonable time for more than one-third of the clergy ordained." Consequently thousands of curates and poor incumbents were condemned to poverty.[39] In the case of assistant curates the discomforts of penury were compounded by insecurity of tenure, by the humiliation of being treated as inferiors by the incumbents for whom they labored, and by the lack of representation in convocation.[40]

The slim chance of achieving relief from these circumstances by promotion to an adequately endowed living was further narrowed for huge numbers of poor clergy by the haphazard method of appointment. Private patrons controlled nearly half the benefices of England. Edward Bartrum, author of a pamphlet entitled *Promotion by Merit Essential to the Progress of the Church* (1866) estimated that at least one-half of the 6,245 livings in private patronage were "obtained by purchase or given away from interested motives"; he found that in 1,290 of those livings the names of patrons and incumbents were the same. Bartrum's investigation also showed that livings in private patronage were worth more, and were located in more desirable areas (not often "in the midst of large and populous districts") than were livings in episcopal or public gift. A clergyman without interest was at a great disadvantage unless he were sufficiently wealthy to buy an advowson and install himself in his own benefice.[41]

The irrationalities of private patronage were compounded by the activities of public patrons of various sorts. Benefices controlled by the crown and by collegiate and cathedral bodies were normally handed out on the basis of connection rather than pastoral accomplishment.[42] A few hundred livings were in the hands of trustees, some of whom, like the Simeon trustees, were conscientious in appointing men of suitable professional qualificiations.[43] In the 1830s and 1840s some writers expressed the hope that bishops could be counted on to use their limited patronage to reward the labors of hard working curates. Certainly a few bishops (Samuel Wilberforce and John Lonsdale were outstanding) took care to do justice to meritorious clergy in making appointments to livings. However, on 21 February 1855 the *Guardian* asserted that episcopal preferment was normally "disposed of from motives which exclude merit of every sort," and on 9 September 1863 it still complained that too many of the best episcopal livings were given to members of the bishops' own families. Trollope stated flatly in 1866 that the bishops exercised their patronage consistently "with the undeniable and acknowledged view of benefiting private friends." For these reasons Edward Bartrum rejected an increase of episcopal patronage as a way of increasing the opportunities for men of merit to advance in the church.[44]

There is plenty of evidence that this complex web of interest and connection was unacceptable to very many clergy in the mid-Victorian Church of England. It was unacceptable because it relegated some clergy to perpetual poverty, because it discouraged able men who were without connection or wealth from entering the ministry, because it neglected professional merit in selecting men for the more responsible charges and offices in the church, and because it often resulted in clergymen being situated in unsuitable posts. In short, the traditional policy of patronage and promotion was condemned by many clergymen for distinctly professional reasons.

The extent of poverty among assistant curates was recognized long before mid-century; and to lessen it the typical Victorian remedy of voluntary charity had been applied as early as 1836. In that year the Church Pastoral Aid Society was formed to supplement the stipends of Evangelical curates. In the following year the Additional Curates' Society was founded to do the same for high church curates. Thirty years later the Curates' Augmentation Fund was established to aid curates who had served without promotion for fifteen years. Not all the victims of clerical poverty were content with this sort of thing, and there must have been many who shared the frustration of one curate who, during a discussion on "Stipendiary Curates" at the 1867 church congress, cried out "I am sick of compassion."[45]

Some in the church sought a cure that went beyond charity, and suggestions were made for a redistribution of clerical income both on the local and diocesan levels. The author of *The Whole Case of the Unbeneficed Clergy* [1843], for example, argued that one-third of the value of a benefice should be assigned to the support of the assistant curate if one was employed. A similar scheme was proposed in 1858 incorporating a sliding scale which varied according to the population of the parish, and the year before, a Liverpool curate put forward the idea of a "general fund" to raise curates' salaries to a reasonable level.[46] None of these ideas resulted in any action. Proposals for reducing the rewards of highly-paid clergy in order to raise the incomes of curates and poor incumbents foundered on the fear that abolishing "prizes" would discourage gentlemen from entering the ministry.[47]

Efforts to reform the promotion practices of the church gained more support among clerical writers than did proposals to re-distribute income. "Prizes" must remain, but they should be "actually achieved by merit," said T. E. Espin, and not "bestowed . . . from nepotism or favouritism or caprice." To start with, a clergyman should have had several years' experience as an assis-tant curate before being promoted to a benefice.[48] This was a preliminary requirement only, for there was much to pastoral merit that could not be guaranteed by experience alone. A large capacity for hard work, energy, and pastoral skill were vital qualities which must be judged objectively and competitively, in some manner comparable to that being introduced into the civil and military services. If a system of appointment and promotion of this sort were introduced into the church,

> incumbents of small livings would work them thoroughly, in the hope of being called up to a higher place. Curates would be more diligent in visiting, more attractive in their preach-ing, more earnest . . . in improving themselves and others, if they were *more certain* of promotion when they deserved it. Interest and duty, duty and interest, would be identified.[49]

Those who condemned interest and connection and called for promotion by merit rarely made precise proposals for change. Edward Bartrum was an exception. He put forward a detailed scheme for the purchase of private patronage by the ecclesiastical commissioners over a period of seventy years. He recommended that a board of trustees should be appointed to select a new incumbent whenever a living was redeemed. It would consist of two churchwardens (to represent "local interest and local wants"), a representative of the ecclesiastical commission (who might serve as chairman of all such boards in a given diocese), a nominee of the diocesan bishop (preferably a layman), and a representative of the local deanery. Bartrum thought that a board thus constituted would be far more likely "to put the right man in the right place" than would a private patron. No totally inexperienced clergyman would receive a living, for no candidate who had not at least three years' experience as an assistant curate could be considered by the appointing trustees. Once the reform was complete, Bartrum calculated that over three hundred livings a year would be open to clergy of proved professional competence whose opportunities would no longer be narrowed by the limitations of connection and wealth.[50]

Considerable as was the cry for reform in the church's methods of appointment and promotion, the barrier of the patronage system proved impassable. A critical problem for reformers was the absence of any sort of powerful central (or even diocesan) authority in patronage matters. Even if such an authority had existed, in the mid-Victorian climate of opinion it would have had difficulty interfering effectively with the free working of the patronage market. Furthermore a good many churchmen believed that the diffusion of patronage among a multitude of private individuals, bishops, and public bodies was beneficial as it assured both variety of clerical opinion within dioceses as well as security and independence for individual parsons.[51] There were also those who thought that a system of appointment and promotion based on merit was inappropriate to this uniquely sacred vocation. "The best clergymen," stated a writer in the *Contemporary Review* in 1866, "are often those who are least likely, not seldom those who are least anxious, to move upwards."[52]

It was not only the management of upward movement in the profession that disturbed Victorian critics of the church's patronage system. The haphazard method of appointment, the security of the parson's freehold, and the absence of any regular method of changing cures, made it likely that a clergyman would find himself in an unsuitable post from which he could neither extricate himself nor be removed. "We send a man with a weak voice to a large church," said a speaker at the 1866 church congress, "a learned divine to an uneducated flock, a half-trained preacher to a congregation which could appreciate and profit by high culture in its minister."[53] In the absence of rational personnel arrangements "the church of this nineteenth century, the century of free trade and division of labour, still digs with a razor and shaves with a spade."[54] Even good appointments could last too long for the welfare of either parson or people. Harry Jones was certain that it was far better for a man to have several pastoral charges during his ministry than to accept a living after college and simply "settle down for life over the cesspool of his own mistakes." In the case of particularly hard cures, especially urban slum parishes, the need for a restricted term was obvious. Just as a soldier was expected to spend only a limited time in a remote colony, so a slum clergyman "who has occupied for a time the position of 'forlorn hope' in the battle of civilisation and religion" should be relieved by a change of post, though not necessarily by a promotion.[55]

The end of far too many clerical careers was spent either in unbeneficed poverty or in beneficed senility. Unless he possessed a private income (as a good many clergymen certainly did) or had won in the lottery for the church's prize appointments, the ordinary pastor had no financial security in retirement except charity. Opportunities for saving toward a retirement income were available in the latter part of the century, but such saving was often impossibly difficult for underpaid curates or poor incumbents. Poor incumbents could keep their incomes by retaining their freeholds even after they had become incapable of fulfilling more than minimal clerical duties. Although this might solve the financial problem of "decayed clergymen," it created a crisis for their parishes, too often leaving "the church neglected, education at a discount, missionary work at a standstill, Dissent rampant, and the love of many waxing cold."[56]

Like all the problems of professional personnel management in the mid-Victorian church, that of aged and disabled clergy inspired a good deal of discussion but very little action other than the application of the traditional nostrums of charity.[57] In 1857 a committee of the upper house of the Canterbury Convocation recommended "a system of recognised resignation of their benefices by incumbents who are no longer able to give their full energies to the work of the ministry," and suggested that pensions should be assigned from the benefices so resigned.[58] Nothing came of this for fourteen years, and when two Incumbents' Resignation Acts (1871 and 1887) were passed by parliament, they did not work well. Neither the convocation proposal nor the subsequent legislation attempted to deal with the plight of aged assistant curates. No effective move was made to provide a regular system of clergy pensions until the twentieth century.[59]

The plight of elderly pastors was a particularly poignant sign that the Victorian church found it difficult to cope with its clergy as professional men. Many other signs have been rehearsed on the pages of this book. Churchmen were unable to enforce acceptable

116

standards of theological knowledge or pastoral training; they could not agree on equitable and practical procedures for clerical appointment and promotion; nor could they find means to adjust the social character of the ministry to the requirements of modern industrial society. Such developments were sometimes resisted on the lofty ground that the ordained ministry was uniquely sacred and ought not to be treated in any respect as an ordinary profession. Yet discussion of professional standards, the search for appropriate forms of professional training, and the emergence of more distinctively clerical styles of life were prominent features of the Victorian church, especially evident in the work of contemporary pastoral theologians. One important reason why effective policies to deal with these matters were not generated was the diffusion of power in the church, the lack of an autonomous authoritative policy making body able to enforce its decisions throughout the institution. Another was the partial subordination of clerical personnel management to lay control, that of crown and parliament, often of trustees or lay patrons as well, and the confusion of this lay element with the powers of individual bishops.

Many aspects of Anglican ecclesiastical life in the last century were dominated by party warfare, by differences and disputes between Evangelicals and Anglo-Catholics, between broad churchmen and biblical conservatives, or between traditional Tory-Anglicans on the one hand and Christian radicals and socialists on the other. This was not the case in the central activity of the Victorian church, the provision of pastoral care for the people of England. Although the distinctive emphases of church parties are evident in contemporary manuals of pastoral theology, they are far from dominant. On most matters the advice given by Evangelicals and Anglo-Catholics, by high or broad churchmen, was strikingly unaffected by the peculiarities of party opinion. This suggests that ordinary Englishmen in ordinary parishes received pastoral care which was little touched by the disputes of churchmanship, that they were not greatly affected by the party controversies which have colored the historiography of nineteenth-century Anglicanism.

The literature of the nineteenth-century pastoral revival was characterized more by a developing professional ideology than by ecclesiastical party controversy. At the core of this ideology was the assumption that the ordained ministry of the Church of England was a religious vocation. Upon this vocation professional character and competence had to be built. To fulfill his calling the ideal ordinand not only had to learn methods and techniques of pastoral care; he also had to become a new person, a different kind of gentlemen, set apart from the rest of mankind by a distinct and elevated style of life. Just as this professional character was peculiarly moral and spiritual, so his professional work was held to be essentially religious. Although the ideal priest might undertake various secular tasks, he would do so frequently for professional reasons and most often from religious motives.

Although the outline of this ideology was clear by 1870 there was uncertainty, confusion, and disagreement (some of it related to differences in churchmanship) about details. Furthermore, the fulfillment of professional aims was often foiled by elements in contemporary church organization, tradition, and practice. The pastoral theologians, the ideologues of clerical professionalization, never overcame these inhibitions, nor did they form anything like a united school or pressure group within the church. Except for those who made names for themselves in other connections, they have been forgotten by historians. Yet they were important figures in revitalizing the parish ministry in nineteenth-century England, and their works are full of ideas about the nature and quality of pastoral care, central themes in Victorian ecclesiastical discussion and debate.

Appendix I

Biographical Notes

BARTRUM, Edward (1834- ?). A graduate of Oxford, he was head master of King Edward's School, Berkhamsted in 1864. He was the author of *Promotion by Merit Essential to the Progress of the Church* (1866).

BAYLEE, Joseph (1808-83). A graduate of Trinity College, Dublin, he was founder and first principal of St. Aidan's Theological College in Birkenhead (1846-68). An Evangelical and a prominent controversialist, he was a strong anti-Catholic and biblical literalist. After leaving Birkenhead (where he was also incumbent of Holy Trinity church) he became vicar of Shepscombe in Gloucestershire.

BEST, Samuel (1802-73). A graduate of Cambridge, he was rector of Abbots-Ann, Andover, from 1831 (the year after he took his M.A.) until his death. He was the author of a number of pamphlets and books, including *A Manual of Parochial Institutions* (1849).

BLUNT, John Henry (1823-84). A graduate of Durham (where he received first a licentiate in theology and afterwards an M.A.), he held curacies and livings in Northumberland, Hampshire, Oxford, and Gloucestershire. A high churchman, he wrote several books and contributed to church periodicals. His handbook *Directorium Pastorale* (1864) came out in at least five editions up to 1875, and was reissued in 1880.

BLUNT, John James (1794-1855). A graduate of Cambridge, he was rector of Great Oakley in Essex from 1834 until his appointment as Lady Margaret Professor of Divinity at Cambridge in 1839. His lectures on pastoral theology were published posthumously as *The Acquirements and Principal Obligations and Duties of the Parish Priest* (1856). This work went through at least four editions.

BRIDGES, Charles (1794-1869). A well-known Evangelical writer and parish clergyman. A graduate of Cambridge, he was vicar of Old Newton in Suffolk from 1823 to 1849, where he wrote his *The Christian Ministry* (1830). One of the most popular of the pastoral handbooks, it came out in eight editions between 1830 and 1854.

BURGON, John William (1813-88). A high churchman and graduate of Oxford, he spent his ministry there until he became dean of Chichester in 1876. While he was vicar of St. Mary's in Oxford he wrote *A Treatise on the Pastoral Office* (1864). He is described in the DNB as "a leading champion of lost causes and impossible beliefs."

CADMAN, William (1815-91). A graduate of Cambridge, he spent most of his ministry in London where he was rector of St. George's, Southwark (1852-59), and of Holy Trinity, Marylebone (1859-91). Also a canon of Canterbury from 1883 to 1891, he was a frequent speaker on aspects of the parish ministry at church congresses in the 1860s.

CHAMPNEYS, William Weldon (1807-75). He was a graduate of Oxford and a prominent Evangelical. After a period as incumbent of St. Ebbe's, Oxford, he served as rector of St. Mary's, Whitechapel, from 1837 to 1860. He moved to St. Pancras in 1860, and eight years later left London to become dean of Lichfield. His handbook *Parish Work* (1866) is based on his London experience.

CLARKE, John Erskine (1828- ?). A graduate of Oxford (where he received his B.A. in 1850), he was appointed vicar of St. Michael's, Derby, in 1859, and he remained there until 1872, when he moved to Battersea. While at Derby he became well-known in the church for his interest in workingmen's recreations, and as a promoter of savings' schemes appropriate for the poor. Editor of several church magazines, he was secretary of the Derbyshire Book-Hawking Union and a director of the Derby Workingmen's Association Penny Bank and of the Derby Savings Bank. He spoke at the church congresses of 1868 and 1869.

CONYBEARE, William John (1815-57). A graduate of Cambridge and first principal of the Liverpool Collegiate Institution (1842-48), he was vicar of Axminster in Devon from 1848 until his death. He was the author of several famous articles on the church in the *Edinburgh Review* during the early fifties.

ESPIN, Thomas Espinelle (1824- ?). A graduate of Oxford and fellow of Lincoln College (1849-54), he held livings in Essex, Cheshire, and Durham. He was appointed Professor of Theology at Queen's College, Birmingham, in 1853; from 1865 to 1873 he was warden of that institution. His writings and speeches at church congresses were principally on the recruitment and education of the clergy.

EVANS, Robert Wilson (1789-1866). A graduate of Cambridge, he was vicar of Tarvin in Cheshire from 1836 to 1842 and of Heversham, Westmoreland, from 1842 until his death. He was archdeacon of Westmoreland from 1856 to 1865. His handbook *The Bishopric of Souls* was based on his Cheshire experience, and was published in five editions between 1842 and 1877.

FRASER, James (1818-85). A graduate of Oxford, he was an authority on education and an exceptionally active bishop of Manchester (1870-85). He was a liberal churchman.

FREEMAN, Philip (1818-75). A Cambridge graduate, where he was a fellow and tutor of Peterhouse (1842-53), he became principal of Chichester Theological College (1846-48), and afterwards Reader in Theology at Cumbrae College in Scotland (1853-58). He ended up as vicar of Thorverton in Devon and a canon and archdeacon of Exeter. His writings and speeches in convocation are about the education of the clergy. He was a high churchman.

GATTY, Alfred (1813-1903). A graduate of Oxford, he served a short curacy before he was appointed vicar of Ecclesfield, near

Sheffield, where he remained for sixty-four years. Well-known for his work on local topography and archaeology, he wrote *The Vicar and His Duties* in 1853.

GIRDLESTONE, Edward (1805-84). A graduate of Oxford, he was appointed vicar of Deane in Lancashire in 1830. In 1858 he moved to Gloucester, and in 1862 became vicar of Halberton in Devon. There he made his reputation as the "agricultural labourer's friend," and aroused the antipathy of the farmers. He proposed an Agricultural Laborers' Union, and actually moved several hundred laborers from the west to the north of England.

GREGORY, Robert (1819-1911). A graduate of Oxford and a high churchman, he was vicar of St. Mary-the-Less in Lambeth for twenty years (1853-73). Appointed a canon of St. Paul's in 1868, he was made dean in 1891.

HOOK, Walter Farquhar (1798-1875). An Oxford graduate, he began his ministry on the Isle of Wight (1821-26), but became well-known for his work in Coventry (1828-37) and especially as vicar of Leeds (1837-59). In 1859 he accepted the deanery of Chichester which he held to his death. He was a high churchman.

HOW, William Walsham (1823-97). A graduate of Oxford and of the theological course at Durham, he was an Anglo-Catholic and became rector of Whittington, Yorkshire, in 1851 where he remained for twenty-eight years. He refused several colonial bishoprics, but became bishop suffragan of Bedford (Diocese of London) in 1879, and bishop of Wakefield in 1888. He wrote extensively on pastoral and devotional topics.

HUME, Abraham (1814-84). Educated at the University of Glasgow and Trinity College, Dublin, he was vicar of All Souls' Vauxhall in Liverpool from 1847 until his death. He is remembered less for his parochial work than for his statistical surveys. See W. S. F. Pickering, "Abraham Hume (1814-1884), A Forgotten Pioneer in Religious Sociology," *Archives de Sociologie des Religions*, no. 33 (1971): 33-48.

JONES, Harry (1823-1900). A Cambridge graduate and a broad churchman, he spent nearly all his ministry in London. After a curacy at St. Mark's, North Audley Steet (1852-57), he was vicar of two slum parishes, St. Luke's, Berwick

Street (1858-72), and St. George's-in-the-East (1873-82). Made a prebendary of St. Paul's Cathedral in 1880, he spent a few years in Suffolk, but returned to London first as vicar of St. Philip's, Regent Street, and finally as rector of St. Vedast's, Foster Lane (1897-1900). Among his many publications was *Priest and Parish* (1866).

LIDDON, Henry Parry (1829-90). An Oxford man and a leading disciple of Keble and Pusey, he was vice-principal of the theological college at Cuddesdon from 1854 to 1859, and afterwards vice-principal of St. Edmund's Hall and Ireland Professor of Exegesis at Oxford. In 1870 he was made a canon of St. Paul's. His various sermons on the education and life of clergymen were published posthumously as *Clerical Life and Work* (1894).

LLOYD, Henry Robert (1809-80). Nephew of Archbishop Longley and graduate of Cambridge, he had several pastoral charges in Wales and southern England. He preached a sermon on *The Responsibilities and Requirements of the Clergy* (1857).

LYTTELTON, William Henry (1820-84). A liberal-minded clergyman and a graduate of Cambridge, he was rector of Hagley, Worcestershire, for nearly all of his ministry (1847-80). A vice-president of the Worcestershire Union of Educational Institutes, he was much interested in schools and the recreations of the poor. He was canon of Gloucester from 1880 until his death.

MACKENZIE, Henry (1808-78). A graduate of Oxford and friend of F. D. Maurice, he spent most of his early ministry in London where he was rector of St. Martin-in-the-Fields from 1848 to 1855. He moved to the Diocese of Lincoln, where he was rector of Tydd St. Mary, and afterwards a canon of Lincoln (1864) and archdeacon of Nottingham (1866). In 1870 he was consecrated bishop suffragan of Nottingham. Among his published works are his *Ordination Lectures* (1862).

MONRO, Edward (1815-66). An Oxford graduate and much influenced by the Tractarian movement, he was perpetual curate of Harrow Weald (1842-60), and vicar of St. John's, Leeds (1860-66), and was well-known both for his stories and his work on pastoral care (especially *Parochial Work* [1850]).

See Brian Heeney, "Tractarian Pastor: Edward Monro of Harrow Weald," *Canadian Journal of Theology*, XIII, no. 4 (1967): 242-51 and XIV, no. 1 (1968): 13-27.

OXENDEN, Ashton (1808-92). An Evangelical and an Oxford graduate, he spent his entire English ministry in Kent, where he was rector of Pluckley from 1849 to 1869. He was bishop of Montreal (1869-78), but returned to become vicar of St. Stephen's, Canterbury, in 1879. The author of an enormous number of tracts and devotional works, he wrote his handbook *The Pastoral Office* in 1857; a new edition was published in 1859.

PYCROFT, James (1813-95). An Oxford man, he studied law and taught for a short time in Leicester. He was incumbent of St. Mary Magdalen, Barnstable (1845-56), after which he did no further clerical duty, but, in the words of the DNB "devoted his time to literature and his leisure to cricket." His *Twenty Years in the Church* (1859) went through four editions.

REICHEL, Charles Parsons (1816-94). A graduate of Trinity College, Dublin, he held various Irish parishes and academic posts. He was consecrated bishop of Meath in 1885. He wrote on "University Reform in Relation to Theological Study" in the first volume of the *Contemporary Review* (1866).

RIDLEY, Henry Colborne (1780-1832). An Oxford graduate who was rector of Hambledon, Bucks, from 1804 until his death. He was credited by Charles Bridges as the author of *Parochial Duties Practically Illustrated* (2nd ed., 1829).

ROWSELL, Thomas James (1816-94). A Cambridge graduate, he spent his life in London parishes: St. Peter's, Stepney (1844-60); St. Margaret's, Lothbury (1860-72); St. Stephen's, Westbourne Park (1872-83). He was a canon of Westminster from 1880 and a member of the broad church Curates' Clerical Club.

SANDFORD, John (1801-73). A Scot, he attended Glasgow University and Oxford, and held the livings of Chillingham (1827-36), Dunchurch (1836-54), Hallow and Alvechurch (1854-?). He was appointed archdeacon of Coventry in 1851. A strong advocate of the temperance cause, he spoke frequently in the lower house of convocation, and wrote *Parochialia* in 1845. He was a friend of Archbishop Tait.

SPOONER, Edward (1821-99). An Oxford graduate, he was vicar of Heston (1859-75) and of Hadleigh (1875-99), and was the author of *Parson and People, or Incidents in the Everyday Life of a Clergyman* (1863).

THOMPSON, Henry (1797-1878). A Cambridge man, he held several livings in southern England and wrote *Pastoralia. A Manual of Helps for the Parish Clergy* (1830).

VAUGHAN, Charles John (1816-97). A pupil of Arnold's at Rugby and a Cambridge graduate, he was headmaster of Harrow (1844-59), vicar of Doncaster (1860-69), master of the Temple (1869-97), and dean of Llandaff from 1879. His activity in preparing ordinands for the work of the ministry (over 450 between 1860 and his death) is described in the DNB as "the most distinctive work of his life."

WHATELY, Richard (1787-1863). An Oxford graduate and a friend of Thomas Arnold, he was a Fellow of Oriel. After being Drummond Professor of Political Economy at Oxford (1829-31), he became archbishop of Dublin in 1831. He was author of a great many printed works, including *The Parish Pastor* (1860).

WILBERFORCE, Henry William (1807-73). Youngest son of William Wilberforce and brother of Samuel, he was a pupil of Newman's at Oriel College, Oxford. After holding three livings in the Church of England, he became a Roman Catholic in 1850. He wrote *The Parochial System* (1838).

WILBERFORCE, Samuel (1805-73). Third son of William Wilberforce and a graduate of Oxford, he was for ten years rector of Brighstone on the Isle of Wight (1830-40), where he wrote *The Notebook of a Country Clergyman* (1833). After serving as archdeacon of Surrey, canon of Winchester, and rector of Alverstoke in Hampshire, he was briefly dean of Westminster before being consecrated bishop of Oxford in 1845. He was translated to Winchester in 1869. His *Addresses to the Candidates for Ordination* was published in 1860.

WILSON, Daniel (1805-86). An Oxford graduate and prominent Evangelical clergyman who was vicar of Islington from 1832 until the end of his life. He was rural dean from 1860, and a prebendary of St. Paul's from 1872.

Appendix II

Number and Sources of Ordinands, England and Wales, 1841-1868

	1841	1850	1851	1852	1853	1854	1855	1856	1857	1858
Oxford	242	211	215	199	211	203	169	171	195	179
Cambridge	270	252	222	234	231	187	225	215	208	222
Durham	13	21	23	27	21	27	29	30	22	32
Dublin	33	50	41	38	41	30	40	40	51	29
Literate*	48	88	113	104	128	77	99	120	130	133
Total	606	622	614	602	632	524	562	576	606	595

	1859	1860	1861	1862	1863	1864	1865	1866	1867	1868
Oxford	181	162	159	120	149	178	169	187	174	181
Cambridge	257	227	219	178	190	194	187	200	200	202
Durham	25	16	21	13	17	8	13	11	14	20
Dublin	29	29	30	32	40	27	32	41	33	30
Literate*	123	133	141	146	120	146	158	149	140	167
Total	615	567	570	489	516	553	559	588	561	600

From: Thomas E. Espin, *Our Want of Clergy, Its Causes and Suggestions for Its Cure* (London 1863), p. 21, and Thomas E. Espin, *Church Congress Report* (1869) p. 63.

*Used in this context to mean "all persons qualified for ordination through other means than graduation at the universities of Oxford, Cambridge, Durham or Dublin".

Espin, Church Congress Report (1869), p. 63.

NOTES

Abbreviations

CC	Chronicle of Convocation (Canterbury)
CCC	Curates' Clerical Club
CCR	Church Congress Report
CO	*Christian Observer*
CR	*Contemporary Review*
CRem	*Christian Remembrancer*
DNB	*Dictionary of National Biography*
ER	*Edinburgh Review*
G	*Guardian*
OCA	Oxford Clerical Association
PP	Parliamentary Papers
QR	*Quarterly Review*

1. Jeremy Bentham, *The Handbook of Political Fallacies,* Harper Torchbook ed. (New York, 1962), pp. 38-41.

2. J. H. Rigg, *The Relations of John Wesley and of Wesleyan Methodism to the Church of England* (London, 1868), p. 8.

3. Edward Miall, *The Nonconformist's Sketch Book,* new ed. (London, 1867), pp. 57-58. Edward Miall (1809-81) was an Independent minister and politican who championed the cause of disestablishment in the Church of England. In 1841 he founded the *Nonconformist* newspaper in which he wrote weekly articles denouncing the state church; these were reprinted as *The Nonconformist's Sketch Book.* Miall was the principal founder of the British Anti-State Church Association (1844) which, in 1853, became the famous Liberation Society, a powerful radical dissenting lobby within the Gladstonian Liberal party. Miall was a member of parliament for Rochdale (1852-57) and for Bradford (1869-74). In the words of the DNB: "Apart from the question of disestablishment Miall had few interests and sought few distractions."

4. *The National* (1839). From Harold U. Faulkner, *Chartism and the Churches* (New York, 1916), p. 29. Also see Eric J. Evans, "Some Reasons for the Growth of English Rural Anticlericalism, c. 1750—c. 1830," *Past and Present* LXVI (February 1975).

5. Eric J. Hobsbawm and George Rudé, *Captain Swing,* Penguin ed. (London, 1973), p. 194. John P. D. Dunbabin, *Rural Discontent in Nineteenth-Century Britain* (London, 1974), p. 248.

6. Anthony Trollope, *Clergymen of the Church of England* (London, 1866), chapter V.

7. Chapter 2, pp. 14ff.

8. Anthony John Russell, "A Sociological Analysis of the Clergyman's Role with Special Reference to Its Development in the Early Nineteenth Century" (D. Phil. thesis, Oxford University, 1970), pp. 3, 498-500.

9. William Cadman, *Church Congress Report* (1861), p. 110; J. B. McCaul, CCR (1865), p. 106; John W. Burgon, *A Treatise on the Pastoral Office, Addressed Chiefly to Candidates for Holy Orders or to Those Who Have Recently Undertaken the Cure of Souls* (London, 1864), pp. 406-7.

10. *Clerical Recreations: Thoughts for the Clergy by One of Themselves* (London, 1863), p. 4; QR, CII (1857): 464.

11. Robert W. Evans, *The Bishopric of Souls* (London, 1842), p. 121; Ashton Oxenden, *The Pastoral Office: Its Duties, Difficulties, Privileges and Prospects* (London, 1857), p. 210; W. Walsham How, *Lectures on Parochial Work Delivered in The Divinity School Cambridge, 1883,* 2d ed. (London, 1884), p. 108.

12. Oxenden, *Pastoral Office,* p. 210; John Stoughton, *Religion in England from 1800 to 1850,* 2 vols. (London, 1884), I: 159; William R. W. Stephens, *The Life and Letters of Walter Farquhar Hook,* 7th ed. (London, 1885), pp. 98, 438-39; Edward Monro, *Parochial Work* (London, 1850), p. 4; *Clerical Recreations,* p. 5; Richard Durnford, CCR (1866), p.

176; John Sandford, *Parochialia, or Church, School and Parish* (London, 1845), pp. viiff.

13. QR, CII: 468. The Reverend Whitwell Elwin was editor of the *Quarterly*, 1853-60.

14. Norman Sykes, *Church and State in England in the Eighteenth Century* (Cambridge, 1934).

15. Friederick W. B. Bullock, *A History of Training for the Ministry of the Church of England in England and Wales from 1800 to 1874* (St. Leonard's-on-Sea, 1955), pp. 10ff.

16. A. R. Humphreys, *The Augustan World*, 2d ed. (London, 1964), pp. 138ff.

17. George S. R. Kitson Clark, *Churchmen and the Condition of England* (London, 1973), pp. 46-47.

18. See the analysis and discussion of pastoral renewal and of its place in the early Victorian revival of the established church in A. D. Gilbert, "The Growth and Decline of Nonconformity in England and Wales with Special Reference to the Period before 1850: An Historical Interpretation of Statistics of Religious Practice" (D. Phil. thesis, Oxford University, 1973), pp. 339ff. Gilbert considers the 1840s to be the crucial years (p. 352).

Notes to Chapter II

1. Oxenden, *Pastoral Office*, p. 41.

2. Charles Bridges, *The Christian Ministry; with an Enquiry into the Causes of Its Inefficiency: with an Especial Reference to the Ministry of the Establishment*, 6th ed. (London, 1844), pp. 182-83.

3. Samuel Wilberforce, *Addresses to the Candidates for Ordination on the Questions of the Ordination Service*, 2d ed. (London, 1860), p. 210; John Sandford, *The Mission and Extension of the Church at Home* (London, 1862), pp. 116-17.

4. Edward Monro, *Sermons Principally on the Responsibilities of the Ministerial Office* (Oxford, 1850), pp. 48-49; Bridges, *Christian Ministry*, p. 26; *Christian Observer* (March 1857), p. 150.

5. Oxenden, *Pastoral Office*, pp. 8, 297; Henry E. Manning, *A Charge Delivered at the Ordinary Visitation of the Archdeaconry of Chichester in July 1846* (London, 1846), p. 25. See Samuel Butler's characterization of the Victorian clergyman as a "kind of human Sunday" in *The Way of All Flesh*, chapter 26.

6. W. Walsham How, "Private Life and Ministrations of the Parish Priest," *The Church and the Age: Essays on the Principles and Present Position of the Anglican Church*, ed. A. Weir and W. D. Maclagan (London, 1870), p. 211.

7. Evans, *Bishopric of Souls*, p. 233; *Clerical Recreations*, p. 10; George Huntington, *Amusements and the Need of Supplying Healthy Recreations for the Poor*, 2d ed. (Oxford, 1868), pp. 32-33; How, "Private Life," p. 211; Harry Jones, *Priest and Parish* (London, 1866), pp. 258ff.; Standish Meacham, *Lord Bishop: The Life of Samuel Wilberforce, 1805-1873* (Cambridge, Mass., 1970), p. 103.

8. Jones, *Priest and Parish*, p. 264; *Clerical Recreations*, pp. 11-12.

9. Evans, *Bishopric of Souls*, p. 216; *Clerical Recreations*, p. 104.

10. Oxenden, *Pastoral Office*, pp. 54, 246-47.

11. *The Deficient Supply of Well-Qualified Clergymen for the Church of England at the Present Time* (Birkenhead, 1863), pp. 13-14.

12. Cecil Wray, *Four Years of Pastoral Work, Being a Sketch of the Ministerial Labours of the Reverend Edward John Rees Hughes* (London, 1854), pp. xi-xii; Henry R. Lloyd, *The Responsibilities and Requirements of the Clergy* (Durham, 1857), p. 21. For differences between Evangelical and Tractarian styles of clerical dress, see Owen Chadwick, *The Victorian Church*, 2 vols. (London, 1966 and 1970), I: 448.

13. For the Henrietta Street club see brochure and list of members under "Clerical Club" in the Bodleian Library. Also see *Guardian*, 18 and 25 August 1858, 18 April and 2 May 1866.

14. Lloyd, *Responsibilities*, p. 20.

15. 6 George IV, c. 50, s. 2; 41 George III, c. 63; 1 and 2 Victoria, c. 106, s. 29. See also *Chronicle of Convocation* (Canterbury, 1859), p. 54; W. H. Pinnock, *The Laws and Usages of the Church and Clergy* (Cambridge, 1855-63), pp. 82, 181ff.; Chadwick, *Victorian Church*, I: 136-37; William R. Ward, *Religion and Society in England 1790-1850* (London, 1972), p. 107.

16. Oxenden, *Pastoral Office*, pp. 24-25; Wilberforce, *Addresses*, p. 4; Edward Monro, *The Fulfilment of the Ministry* (London, 1848), p. 9; Oxford Clerical Association Minute Books, 2 February 1863.

17. Joseph Baylee, *Theological Colleges: Their True Use and Their Important Bearing Upon the Theological Education of the Clergy* (London, 1855), p. 3; James Pycroft, *Twenty Years in the Church: An Autobiography*, 4th ed. (London, 1861), p. 151; Wilberforce, *Addresses*, p. 222.

18. W. H. Hale, *The Duties of Deacons and Priests in the Church of England Compared: With Suggestions for the Extension of the Order of Deacons and the Establishment of an Order of Sub-Deacons* (London, 1850) and W. H. Hale, *Suggestions for the Extension of the Ministry and the Revival of the Order of Sub-Deacons: A Charge Delivered to the Clergy of the Archdeaconry of London, May 24, 1852* (London, 1852); CC (1859), pp. 54-55.

19. CCR (1867), p. 315.

20. Jones, *Priest and Parish*, pp. 82, 250. Also see Edward Monro, *The Navvies and How to Meet Them* (London, 1857), pp. 21ff.; and G, 16 February 1865.

21. CCR (1863), p. 177. On Cadman's use of lay pastoral helpers, see chapter III. p. 59.

22. Sandford, *Parochialia*, p. 220; Alfred Gatty, *The Vicar and His Duties* (London, 1853), p. 27.

23. Edward Monro, *Pastoral Life* (London, 1862), p. 53; Evans, *Bishopric of Souls*, p. 284; Wilberforce, *Addresses*, p. 124; Henry Mackenzie, *Ordination Lectures, delivered in Riseholme Palace Chapel During Ember Weeks* (London, 1862), p. 79.

24. Pycroft, *Twenty Years*, pp. 110-11. See also Jones, *Priest and Parish*, p. 21; Monro, *Pastoral Life*, p. 69; Edward Spooner, *Parson and People, or Incidents in the Everyday Life of a Clergyman*, 2d ed. (London, 1864), pp. 204-5; How, "Private Life," p. 213. For an example of a scheme to induce systematic parochial work, see J. B. Sweet, *Speculum Parochiale, According to a Form Prepared by J. B. Sweet* (London, 1859).

25. CCR (1865), p. 110.

26. Charles Richard Sumner, *A Charge Delivered to the Clergy of the Diocese of Winchester* (London, 1862), p. 18. Also see Bridges, *Christian Ministry*, pp. 145ff.; John H. Blunt, *Directorium Pastorale. Principles and Practice of Pastoral Work in the Church of England* (London, 1864), pp. 67-68, 98.

27. Pycroft, *Twenty Years*, pp. 149-50. Bernard Shaw sketched a late Victorian Christian Socialist model of such an activist priest as James Morell in *Candida* (1895).

28. Oxenden, *Pastoral Office*, p. 13; Pycroft, *Twenty Years*, p. 170; Edward Monro, *The Parish* (Oxford, 1853), pp. 41-42; Wilberforce, *Addresses*, p. 224; Stephens, *Hook*, p. 503. On the other hand Trollope thought "something approaching hypocrisy" was a "necessary component part of the character of the English parish parson" (*Clergymen*, p. 63).

29. Monro, *Sermons*, p. 7; Oxenden, *Pastoral Office*, p. 183; *Hints to Young Clergymen* (London, n.d. [1874]), p. 10.

30. Trollope, *Clergymen*, pp. 62-63. On the matter of the different expectations which different people and classes had of the parson, see Russell, "Sociological Analysis," chapter 14.

31. *Edinburgh Review*, IC (January 1854), pp. 109-110.

32. CC (1860), pp. 130, 132-33. See Geoffrey F. A. Best, *Temporal Pillars: Queen Anne's Bounty, The Ecclesiastical Commissioners and The Church of England* (Cambridge 1964), p. 399.

33. Bridges, *Christian Ministry*, p. 360; Henry Mackenzie, *Service, not Rule, the Work of the Ministry* (London, 1856), pp. 6-7. Also see QR, CXI (April 1862): 402; CCR (1869), p. 149; Olive Anderson, "The Growth of Christian Militarism in Mid-Victorian Britain," *English Historical Review*, LXXXVI, (January, 1971): 69ff.

34. Blunt, *Directorium Pastorale*, p. 5.

35. Speech by Canon Stowell in CCR (1863), p. 64. Also see speech by Canon Gray in CCR (1869), p. 52; Diana McClatchey, *Oxfordshire Clergy, 1777-1869* (Oxford, 1960), p. 25.

36. Burgon, *Treatise*, p. 239. Also see McClatchey, *Oxfordshire Clergy*, p. 231.

37. A. Tindal Hart, *Clergy and Society, 1600-1800* (London, 1968), p. 63. Most, in fact, were graduates. The most famous statement of the low social status of the Restoration clergy is in the third chapter of Macaulay's

History of England. It provoked violent response from Victorian Tories; but despite some inaccuracies, Macaulay's account is now accepted as substantially accurate. See Sir Charles Firth, *A Commentary on Macaulay's History of England* (London, 1964), pp. 129-32.

38. McClatchey, *Oxfordshire Clergy*, p. 111; Evans, "Rural Anticlericalism," pp. 85-101.

39. James A. Froude, "Reminiscences of the High Church Revival," *Good Words* (1881), p. 20.

40. ER, XCVII (April 1853): 348-49, 360.

41. A. Tindal Hart, *The Curate's Lot* (London, 1971), pp. 130-31.

42. Trollope, *Clergymen*, p. 68. On the social origins of Leeds clergy, see Charles M. Elliott, "The Social and Economic History of the Principal Protestant Denominations in Leeds, 1760-1844" (D. Phil. thesis, Oxford University, 1962), pp. 385ff.

43. Thomas Arnold, *Principles of Church Reform* (London, 1962), p. 118. On the clergy as social reconcilers, see chapter IV, pp. 68ff.

44. CC (1862), p. 948.

45. Blunt, *Directorium Pastorale*, pp. 85-86.

46. Abraham Hume, *Condition of Liverpool, Religious and Social; Including Notices of the State of Education and Morals, Pauperism and Crime*, 2d ed. (Liverpool, 1858), p. 39; Robert Gregory, *The Difficulties and the Organisation of a Poor Metropolitan Parish, Two Lectures Delivered on the 16th and 17th November 1865 to the Students at the Theological College Cuddesdon* (London, 1866), p. 6.

47. Hume in CCR (1869), p. 358; Gregory, *Difficulties*, pp. 10-11.

48. H. Mackenzie, CC (1862), p. 947; Great Britain, *Parliamentary Papers*, 1857-58, vol. IX, *Report from the Select Committee of the House of Lords Appointed to Inquire into the Deficiency of Means of Spiritual Instruction and Places of Worship in the Metropolis and Other Populous Places in England and Wales, Especially in the Mining and Manufacturing Districts*, p. 423; Bridges, *Christian Ministry*, p. 129.

49. In the decade 1851-61 the population of England and Wales increased by about one-eighth and the number of clergy by about one-eleventh; in the decade 1861-71 the population increased by nearly one-seventh and the number of clergy rose by about one-twelfth (Chadwick, *Victorian Church*, II: 244; Brian R. Mitchell and Phyllis Deane, *Abstract of British Historical Statistics* [Cambridge, 1962], p. 6). A contemporary observer, T. E. Espin, recorded much more pessimistic figures, probably because he excluded nonparochial clergy: "In 'Parker's Church Calendar' for 1863, the benefices of England and Wales are returned as in number 12,023, curates as 4,930. In the 'Clerical Guide' for 1829 [Rivingtons] the benefices are 10,719, the curates 5,232. The totals will be 15,951 for 1829, and 16,953 for 1863. In the meantime the population had increased from 13,896,797 in 1831, to 20,209,671 in 1861" (Thomas E. Espin, *Our Want of Clergy, Its Causes and Suggestions for Its Cure* [London, 1863], p. 22).

50. For ordination figures from 1841 to 1868, see appendix II. The 1874 figure was 655; that for 1875 was 614 ("Report of the Committee of the Lower House of Convocation of Canterbury on Deficiencies of Spiritual

Ministration," CC [1876], p. 28). For variant figures from 1872, see Chadwick, II:249, and *Facts and Figures About the Church of England* (London, 1962), section D, table 36.

51. "Report of Committee," p. 9; Chadwick, *Victorian Church*, II:244.

52. On depopulated city parishes, see the evidence of Charles Hume in *PP*, 1857-58, vol. IX, *Spiritual Instruction and Places of Worship*, pp. 269-70. His parish had a real population of 207, and this was steadily decreasing in the mid-Victorian period. On Liverpool, see Ibid., p. 403. On London, see Espin, *Our Want of Clergy*, p. 24. On Newcastle and Bradford, see *PP*, 1857-58, vol. IX, *Spiritual Instruction and Places of Worship*, pp. 407-8, 417-21.

53. See *PP*, 1857-58, vol. IX, *Spiritual Instruction and Places of Worship*, pp. 28, 58, 324, 421. Also see John Davies, *The Subdivision and Rearrangement of Parishes* (London, 1849), p. 17; "Report of Committee," p. 12. T. J. Rowsell of St. Peter's, Stepney, thought that one clergyman for thirty-five hundred or four thousand would be satisfactory; on the other hand a committee of the lower house of convocation recommended a ratio of one to one thousand in 1858 (*PP*, 1857-58, vol. IX, *Spiritual Instruction and Places of Worship*, p. 79; CC [1858], p. 78). Espin showed in 1863 that to effect the ideal ratio of one clergyman to two thousand souls in London alone "requires more than the whole of the clergy who yearly receive ordination" (*Our Want of Clergy*, p. 24). In 1876 a committee of the lower house of Canterbury Convocation calculated that 2,159 additional clergy were needed to achieve the 1/2,000 ratio (CC [1876], p. 12).

54. *Academic Origin of Ordinands*	1851-55	1861-65
Cambridge	1099	949
Oxford	997	783
Dublin	190	150
Durham	127	74
Literates	521	676
Total	2934	2632

From CR, VI (1867):423. *The Oxford Dictionary* defines "literate" as "one who is admitted to holy orders without having obtained a university degree." However its use here is looser, and includes graduates of universities (e. g., London) other than the four specified. Espin, *Our Want of Clergy*, p. 21. Also see appendix II.

55. CRem, XIII (April 1847):291-92; ER, IC (January 1854):94-129; William Ince, *Holy Orders: The Call and the Preparation* (Oxford, 1862), p. 8; CO (January 1863), pp. 46-47; CR, VI (1867):423-26; Edward Bartrum, *Promotion by Merit Essential to the Progress of the Church* (London, 1866), pp. 7ff. See below, chapter V, pp. 111ff.

56. *PP*, 1857-58, vol. IX, *Spiritual Instruction and Places of Worship*, pp. 233, 235; G, 9 September 1863 (letter from "B" and leading article); CCR (1861), p. 127. See also Best, *Temporal Pillars*, p. 447. For a contrasting view of the financial position of the clergy, see H. B. Thomson, *The Choice of a Profession* (London, 1857), pp. 74-75.

57. ER, IC (January 1854):101.

58. CCR (1861), p. 124. See also McClatchey, *Oxfordshire Clergy*, p. 15.

59. CRem, XIII (April 1847):292; CO (January 1863), p. 48; CCR (1863), p. 62; Sandford, *Mission and Extension*, pp. 83-84.

60. C. P. Reichel, "University Reform," CR, I (April 1866):519.

61. T. E. Espin in CCR (1863), pp. 76-77.

62. CRem (1867), pp. 120-22.

63. CC (1863), p. 1223.

64. CCR (1864), p. 201. See also Sandford, *Mission and Extension*, p. 129; CCR (1869), p. 70.

65. Blunt, *Directorium Pastorale*, p. 6.

66. CR, I (April 1866):518.

67. Jones, *Priest and Parish*, p. 12: Mackenzie, *Ordination Lectures*, p. 73.

68. W. J. Conybeare, "Ecclesiastical Economy," ER, IC (January 1854): 105; PP, 1857-58, vol. IX, *Spiritual Instruction and Places of Worship*, p. 221; Jones, *Priest and Parish*, p. 227.

69. Pycroft, *Twenty Years*, p. 277; CCR (1869), p. 52; QR, CIII (1858):139-79.

70. A Tractarian was a special kind of high churchman, one deeply affected by the ideas, attitudes, and practices of the Oxford tract writers and their successors. Although by late in the century most high churchmen had absorbed some Tractarian principle and a good deal of Anglo-Catholic practice this was not true in the period under consideration. Generally, Tractarians (and their successors, the Anglo-Catholics), were less attached to the principle of establishment than were other high churchmen, and were also much less concerned to defend the English Reformation than to stress their attachment to Christian antiquity. The classic differentiation among types of high churchmen in mid-century was made by W. J. Conybeare in the *Edinburgh Review* (October 1853). He described Tractarians as the "exaggerated type" of high churchmen.

Notes to Chapter III

1. For affirmations of the central place of religion in the pastoral vocation, see Bridges, *Christian Ministry*, pp. 9-10; Oxenden, *Pastoral Office*, p. 40; Wilberforce, *Addresses*, pp. 12-13; Monro, *Parochial Work*, pp. 259-60; Philip Freeman, *A Plea for the Education of the Clergy* (London, 1851), p. 40. On the priest's secular work see below, chapter IV.

2. *Clerical Papers by One of Our Club* (London, 1861), pp. 16-17; Jones, *Priest and Parish*, p. 90. Also see Evans, *Bishopric of Souls*, pp. 103ff.; Mackenzie, *Ordination Lectures*, pp. 6-8.

3. See Benjamin Whitehead, *Church Law*, 3d ed. (London, 1911), pp. 258-59.

4. A good many churchmen opposed liturgical change, usually out of

respect for prayer book language or from sheer religious conservatism. For example, John Jebb, rector of Peterstow in Herefordshire, was "convinced . . . that the compilation of our liturgy, and its revision in 1662, were so directly acts of Divine Providence, that it is hardly possible to change a word of our formularies for the better." J. C. Ryle, the Evangelical vicar of Stradbroke in Suffolk, did not believe that Prayer Book forms could be improved; he argued that change was needed in the manner the clergy read the services, not in the matter of the services themselves. CCR (1868), pp. 300, 308. Also see Burgon, *Treatise*, p. 381.

5. Stoughton, *Religion in England*, I:79-80.

6. [H. C. Ridley], *Parochial Duties, Practically Illustrated*, 2d ed. (Henley-on-Thames, 1829), pp. 18-19.

7. On Cadman see *PP*, 1857-58, vol. IX, *Spiritual Instruction and Places of Worship*, p. 149; CCR (1863), p. 179. On Shaftesbury's theater services, see CO (April 1860), p. 279; Randall T. Davidson and William Benham, *Life of Archibald Campbell Tait*, 2 vols. (London, 1891), I:263. On mission services, see Davidson and Benham, *Tait*, I:261; *PP*, 1857-58, vol. IX, *Spiritual Instruction and Places of Worship*, pp. 291ff.; the report of a mission service conducted by Samuel Wilberforce in G, 26 March 1859; speech by W. D. Maclagan in CCR (1869), pp. 371-72. On cathedral popular services, see CC (1857), pp. 79,90; Chadwick, *Victorian Church*, II:381; Davidson and Benham, *Tait*, I:259.

8. CCR (1862), pp. 183-84.

9. CO (December 1856), p. 836; CO (August 1855), p. 509.

10. On Curling, see G, 3 October 1855; on Trench, see G, 31 October 1855; on Molyneux, see G, 25 April 1855; on Bardsley, see CCR (1864), p. 37.

11. Davidson and Benham, *Tait*, I:255; Sumner, *Charge*, p. 8.

12. G, 13 September 1854 and 24 September 1856.

13. Burgon, *Treatise*, p. 172; Jones, *Priest and Parish*, pp. 121, 173-74.

14. McClatchey, *Oxfordshire Clergy*, pp. 84-85.

15. Sandford, *Parochialia*, pp. 247ff.; Jones, *Priest and Parish*, pp. 106-8; Blunt, *Directorium Pastorale*, 1872 ed., p. 48.

16. CRem, XXXIX (1860):469-70; Blunt, *Directorium Pastorale*, pp. 53-54.

17. Monro, *Parochial Work*, p. 66; Sandford, *Parochialia*, p. 251; Blunt, *Directorium Pastorale*, p. 54.

18. Sandford, *Parochialia*, p. 253; *The Parish and the Priest: Colloquies on the Pastoral Care and Parochial Institutions of a Country Village* (London, 1858), p. 18.

19. *PP*, 1857-58, vol. IX, *Spiritual Instruction and Places of Worship*, p. 420; Harry Jones, *Fifty Years or Dead Leaves and Living Seeds* (London, 1895), p. 57; Monro, *Parochial Work*, p. 79.

20. Oxenden, *Pastoral Office*, p. 97; Jones, *Priest and Parish*, p. 126; Monro, *Parochial Work*, pp. 90, 94; Burgon, *Treatise*, p. 168.

21. William W. Champneys, *Parish Work: A Brief Manual for the Younger Clergy* (London, 1866), p. 50; CCR (1865), p. 237.

22. See Wilberforce, *Addresses*, p. 53; CR (January 1867), p. 28; speech

by Daniel Moore in CCR (1865), p. 219; Burgon, *Treatise*, p. 173; Jones, *Priest and Parish*, pp. 128-29.

23. For an example of the Evangelical view, see Oxenden, *Pastoral Office*, p. 107. For the high church view, see Blunt, *Directorium Pastorale*, p. 116; Burgon, *Treatise*, pp. 171, 181.

24. Jones, *Priest and Parish*, pp. 143-44, 146.

25. Wilberforce, *Addresses*, p. 14; Burgon, *Treatise*, p. 186; J. F. Mackarness and R. Seymour, eds., *Eighteen Years of a Clerical Meeting* (London, 1862), p. 223.

26. John J. Blunt, *The Acquirements and Principal Obligations and Duties of the Parish Priest: Being a Course of Lectures Delivered at the University of Cambridge to the Students in Divinity* (London, 1856), pp. 112, 134.

27. Wilberforce, *Addresses*, p. 189; Lloyd, *Responsibilities*, p. 16.

28. Bridges, *Christian Ministry*, p. 49; Oxenden, *Pastoral Office*, pp. 75-76.

29. Jones, *Priest and Parish*, pp. 24, 27-30.

30. Mackenzie, *Ordination Lectures*, p. 71. Also see Burgon, *Treatise*, pp. 178ff.

31. Evans, *Bishopric of Souls*, p. 130; Jones, *Priest and Parish*, p. 136. On sermon length, see Oxenden, *Pastoral Office*, pp. 85, 132; Jones, *Priest and Parish*, p. 133; Burgon, *Treatise*, p. 382; Champneys, *Parish Work*, pp. 50, 63. Oxenden favored between twenty-five and forty-five minutes depending on the style; Jones said that a preacher should never run over twenty minutes; Burgon specified half an hour; Champneys warned against the hour-long sermon.

32. Blunt, *Directorium Pastorale*, p. 121; Jones, *Priest and Parish*, p. 132. On enunciation and throat care, see G, 28 July 1848 (letter from "the incumbent of a large parish").

33. QR, CII (1857):489.

34. Champneys, *Parish Work*, p. 61; [Sewell] QR, CXI (April 1862): 411; Monro, *Parochial Work*, p. 91.

35. Burgon, *Treatise*, pp. 197, 199; Bridges, *Christian Ministry* pp. 286ff.; Jones, *Priest and Parish*, p. 158.

36. Bridges, *Christian Ministry*, p. 206; Oxenden, *Pastoral Office*, p. 90.

37. Blunt, *Directorium Pastorale*, pp. 164, 166; Gatty, *Vicar and his Duties*, p. 51.

38. Mackarness and Seymour, *Eighteen Years*, pp. 146-47. See also Bridges, *Christian Ministry*, p. 451; Monro, *Parochial Work*, p. 103; Burgon, *Treatise*, pp. 345-49.

39. Blunt, *Directorium Pastorale*, p. 162. Also see Sandford, *Parochialia*, p. 266; Wray, *Hughes*, p. 60.

40. Evidence given before a select committee of the House of Lords in the 1850s reveals an enormous number of baptisms in urban parishes. For example, All Saints', Poplar, a parish of twenty-eight thousand people had a "below average" number of five hundred baptisms a year. The incumbent of St. Peter's, Stepney, reported about the same number in a parish population of fourteen thousand. There were over fifteen hundred

in one year at St. Matthew's, Bethnal Green, a parish of only ten thousand souls. See *PP*, 1857-58, vol. IX, *Spiritual Instruction and Places of Worship*, pp. 39, 78, 183. Also see Stephens, *Hook*, p. 222.

41. Sykes, *Church and State*, pp. 115ff.; Arthur Warne, *Church and Society in Eighteenth-Century Devon* (Newton Abbot, 1969), pp. 32-33.

42. Monro, *Parochial Work*, p. 153; Blunt, *Directorium Pastorale*, pp. 177-78.

43. CO (March 1858), p. 151. Also see *Parish and the Priest*, pp. 141ff.

44. Sandford, *Mission and Extension*, p. 153. Speech of Henry Clarke, Esq., in CCR (1868), p. 159.

45. Generally the recommended duration was longer in the later works. See Ridley, *Parochial Duties*, p. 36; Henry Thompson, *Pastoralia. A Manual of Helps for the Parish Clergy* (London, 1830), p. 188; Oxenden, *Pastoral Office*, pp. 223-25; Burgon, *Treatise*, p. 292; Champneys, *Parish Work*, p. 70. Edward Monro, however, felt that group classes were a confession of the failure of religious teaching in elementary day schools (*Parochial Work*, p. 153).

46. Burgon, *Treatise*, pp. 289-90; Blunt, *Directorium Pastorale*, pp. 179-83; Champneys, *Parish Work*, pp. 71-77, 139-54.

47. Bridges, *Christian Ministry*, p. 394; Sandford, *Parochialia*, pp. 268ff.; *Parish and the Priest*, p. 71; Burgon, *Treatise*, pp. 187, 279; Champneys, *Parish Work*, pp. 19-20. On eighteenth-century practice, see Sykes, *Church and State*, pp. 243ff.; Warne, *Church and Society*, pp. 48-49; McClatchey, *Oxfordshire Clergy*, p. 144.

48. Burgon, *Treatise*, p. 295; Stephens, *Hook*, p. 282; *PP*, 1857-58, vol. IX, *Spiritual Instruction and Places of Worship*, pp. 72-73. There was some controversy about the proportion of the population that ought to be confirmed annually. See G, 17 and 24 April 1861, 1 and 8 May 1861.

49. Burgon, *Treatise*, pp. 288, 295; Champneys, *Parish Work*, p. 77; How, "Private Life," p. 221.

50. Champneys, *Parish Work*, p. 78; Burgon, *Treatise*, p. 302; How, "Private Life," p. 221. Also see Blunt, *Directorium Pastorale*, p. 183.

51. On eighteenth-century practice, see Sykes, *Church and State*, pp. 250ff.; Warne, *Church and Society*, p. 45; McClatchey, *Oxfordshire Clergy*, pp. 86ff.; Chadwick, *Victorian Church*, I:515. On the effects of the Evangelical and Oxford movements, see Russell, "Sociological Analysis," pp. 134ff. For evidence of weekly communion in an Evangelical parish by 1859, see the report of Cadman's work in Leonard E. Shelford, *A Memorial to the Reverend William Cadman, M.A.* (London, 1899), p. 61. Champneys, a prominent Evangelical pastoral theologian, had twice-monthly celebrations in his parish during the mid-fifties (*PP*, 1857-58, vol. IX, *Spiritual Instruction and Places of Worship*, p. 133).

52. Oxenden, *Pastoral Office*, pp. 227-28, 230; Burgon, *Treatise*, p. 393.

53. Mackarness and Seymour, *Eighteen Years*, p. 204; Richard Whately, *The Parish Pastor* (London, 1860), p. 275.

54. CRem, IX (1845):464; Mackarness and Seymour, *Eighteen Years*, p. 206.

55. Richard Whately, *The Parochial System: Being the Charge Deliv-*

ered at the *Triennial Visitation of the Province of Dublin* (Dublin, 1859), pp. 11, 17; Bridges, *Christian Ministry,* pp. 382-83; Burgon, *Treatise,* pp. 378ff.

56. In St. Pancras, London, for example, there were 1,522 marriages in the parish church during 1857, including no less than forty-two on Christmas Day (*PP,* 1857-58, vol. IX, *Spiritual Instruction and Places of Worship,* p. 208). See Burgon, *Treatise,* pp. 342-43.

57. Burgon, *Treatise,* p. 365; G, 19 January 1859 (letter from "R. B."). On the threat of cemeteries to pastoral care, see evidence of T. J. Rowsell in *PP,* 1857-58, vol. IX, *Spiritual Instruction and Places of Worship,* p. 74.

58. Mackarness and Seymour, *Eighteen Years,* p. 62; Monro, *Parochial Work,* pp. 42, 53.

59. How, "Private Life," p. 217.

60. Thompson, *Pastoralia,* pp. 97-98; Samuel Wilberforce, *The Notebook of a Country Clergyman* (London, 1833), pp. 133-34.

61. Wilberforce, *Addresses,* pp. 114-15; Burgon, *Treatise,* pp. 217ff.; Blunt, *Directorium Pastorale,* pp. 253-70.

62. Evans, *Bishopric of Souls,* p. 26; Henry Mackenzie, *On the Parochial System as a Means of Alleviating Temporal Distress in the Metropolis* (London, 1850), pp. 8-9.

63. Pycroft, *Twenty Years,* p. 202 (quotation from Dr. Chalmers). See also Monro, *Parochial Work,* p. 158; Jones, *Priest and Parish,* p. 41.

64. Blunt, *Directorium Pastorale,* p. 200; Monro, *Parochial Work,* pp. 161-62.

65. Jones, *Priest and Parish,* p. 51; on the matter of the pastor braving infection, see Wilberforce, *Addresses,* p. 135; Blunt, *Directorium Pastorale,* pp. 222-23; Oxenden, *Pastoral Office,* p. 179.

66. Oxenden, *Pastoral Office,* p. 181; Burgon, *Treatise,* p. 236; Champneys, *Parish Work,* p. 36; Blunt, *Directorium Pastorale,* pp. 211, 195ff.; Wilberforce, *Addresses,* p. 129.

67. Burgon, *Treatise,* p. 217; Jones, *Priest and Parish,* p. 51. Also see Blunt, *Directorium Pastorale,* pp. 195ff. and Champneys, *Parish Work,* pp. 32ff. On superstitious attitudes to Holy Communion in times of sickness, see Oxenden, *Pastoral Office,* pp. 180-81; Abraham Hume, *Missions at Home, or a Clergyman's Account of a Portion of the Town of Liverpool* (London, 1850), p. 17.

68. Oxenden, *Pastoral Office,* p. 184; Monro, *Parochial Work,* p. 162; Blunt, *Directorium Pastorale,* pp. 230, 233ff., 244ff. Also see Burgon, *Treatise,* p. 226; Pinnock, *Laws and Usages,* pp. 99-100; Hume, *Missions at Home,* p. 22; S. Earnshaw, *The Church and the Artisan* (London, 1861), p. 8; Jones, *Priest and Parish,* pp. 38ff.

69. Wilberforce, *Addresses,* p. 116. Also see Evans, *Bishopric of Souls,* pp. 30ff.; Mackenzie, *Ordination Lectures,* pp. 8-9; Burgon, *Treatise,* pp. 226ff.; Blunt, *Directorium Pastorale,* pp. 224-26. For a good example of a pastoral diary, see Sweet, *Speculum Parochiale.*

70. CCR (1865), p. 117; Jones, *Priest and Parish,* p. 201; QR, CIX (April 1861):462.

71. Kenneth S. Inglis, *Churches and the Working Classes in Victorian England* (London, 1963), p. 25; speech by the dean of Chichester (Hook) in CCR (1865), p. 100; Henry W. Wilberforce, *The Parochial System: An Appeal to English Churchmen* (London, 1838), p. 8.

72. Best, *Temporal Pillars*, pp. 195, 354ff.; Inglis, *Churches and the Working Classes*, p. 28; Chadwick, *Victorian Church*, II:241; Gilbert, "Growth and Decline of Nonconformity," Table 7:1, p. 345.

73. Earnshaw, *Church and the Artisan*, pp. 7-9; evidence of W. Rivington in *PP*, 1857-58, vol. IX, *Spiritual Instruction and Places of Worship*, p. 234; CCR (1863), pp. 23-24; CCR (1869), p. 368.

74. Hume, *Condition of Liverpool*, pp. 22-23; Mackenzie, *Parochial System*, p. 13; evidence of Cadman and Dale in *PP*, 1857-58, vol. IX, *Spiritual Instruction and Places of Worship*, pp. 145ff., 211. See above, chapter II, p. 26.

75. *PP*, 1857-58, vol. IX, *Spiritual Instruction and Places of Worship*, p. 166 (King), 256 (Kempe), 264 (Eyre), 147 (Cadman); Mackenzie, *Parochial System*, p. 13.

76. CCR (1862), p. 179; CCR (1863), pp. 179-80; Shelford, *Memorial*, pp. 33ff.

77. CCR (1863), p. 177; Bridges, *Christian Ministry*, pp. 474-75; Jones, *Priest and Parish*, p. 67; CCR (1861), pp. 105ff. (Mackenzie); Gregory, *Difficulties*, pp. 29-36.

78. Benson's statement is in OCA Minute Book 8, (1857), p. 83; CRem, XXVII (1854):409-10, XLIV (1862):462; Blunt, *Directorium Pastorale*, pp. 308ff. For an Evangelical view, see Bridges, *Christian Ministry*, pp. 473ff. On lay roles in the consultative and policymaking life of the church, see CC (1857), pp. 96ff.; CC (1863), pp. 1404-5; Kenneth A. Thompson, *Bureaucracy and Church Reform* (Oxford, 1970), chapter 4. Also see M. J. D. Roberts, "The Role of the Laity in the Church of England, c.1850-1885" (D. Phil. thesis, Oxford University, 1974), pp. 201-24.

79. On sisterhoods see *PP*, 1857-58, vol. IX, *Spiritual Instruction and Places of Worship*, pp. 172ff. (King); Chadwick, *Victorian Church*, I:505ff. On deaconesses, see CO (December 1858), pp. 905ff. and G, 9 December 1863. Also see Roberts, "Role of the Laity," pp. 228ff. Roberts notes that by 1885 there were nine deaconess institutions with sixty full members and two hundred probationers; in the same year there were about thirty sisterhoods and approximately thirteen hundred sisters. For interesting reflections on the differences between sisters and deaconesses, see Alan Deacon and Michael Hill, "The Problem of Surplus Women in the Nineteenth Century: Secular and Religious Alternatives," *A Sociological Yearbook of Religion in Britain* (London, 1972).

80. QR, CIX (April 1861):448-50; Stoughton, *Religion in England*, II:93ff.; Gregory, *Difficulties*, p. 20; *PP*, 1857-58, vol. IX, *Spiritual Instruction and Places of Worship*, pp. 125ff., 146ff. (evidence of Champneys and Cadman).

81. See G, 4 July 1860, 30 January and 20 February 1861. On locally recruited agents, as well as on the comparative costs of male scripture

readers and curates, see *PP*, 1857-58, vol. IX, *Spiritual Instruction and Places of Worship*, Minutes of Evidence. Bible women in 1860 were paid between twelve shillings and sixteen shillings per week (G, 4 July 1860). On the other hand Parochial Church Women were receiving only ten shillings in the early seventies. [C. S. Talbot], *A Servant of the Poor, or Some Account of the Life and Death of a Parochial Mission Woman* (London, 1874), p. 19.

82. *PP*, 1857-58, vol. IX, *Spiritual Instruction and Places of Worship*, p. 187 (Bickersteth); CO (July 1852), p. 439; QR (January 1858), p. 157; CCR (1865), p. 103 (Hook). Also see Spooner, *Parson and People*, pp. 66ff.; CR (September 1866), p. 135.

83. On the knife grinders, see OCA Minute Book 12 (1865), p. 42; CCR (1863), p. 94 (Rowsell); R. Gregory, *Account of the Schools and Charities in Connexion with the District Church of St. Mary-the-Less Lambeth* (London, 1863), p. 11. See also Harry Jones, *Some Grateful Thoughts and Some Grave Anxieties about a London District* (London, 1853), p. 11.

84. Hume, *Condition of Liverpool*, p. 40; for St. Pancras, see Spooner, *Parson and People*, p. 52; for Chelsea, see Shelford, *Memorial*, p. 24. For other evidence of female visitors in London parishes, see *PP*, 1857-58, vol. IX, *Spiritual Instruction and Places of Worship*, Minutes of Evidence. For male participation, ibid., pp. 48ff., 511ff.

85. G, 17 November 1858; [Francis Hessey], *Hints to District Visitors* (London, 1858); Spooner, pp. 52-53; Sandford, *Parochialia*, pp. 379-81.

86. Hessey, *District Visitors*, p. 9. Also see G, 17 November 1858; Champneys, *Parish Work*, p. 29.

Notes to Chapter IV

1. Carl H. E. Zangerl, "The Social Composition of the County Magistracy in England and Wales, 1831-1887," *Journal of British Studies* XI (November 1971):118. Also see Kitson Clark, *Churchmen*, pp. 145-46; McClatchey, *Oxfordshire Clergy*, pp. 178ff.; Evans, "Rural Anticlericalism," pp. 101ff. Another major secular clerical responsibility in pre-Victorian times was administration of the old poor law (Kitson Clark, *Churchmen*, p. 156).

2. Jones, *Priest and Parish*, pp. 215, 217. See also QR, XCVI (December 1854):143; G, 31 October 1855 (letter from "W. W. H."); G, 19 October 1865 (leading article on "Retreats").

3. Thomson, *Choice of a Profession*, p. 91. Also see Sandford, *Parochialia*, p. 205; Evans, *Bishopric of Souls*, p. 26; Burgon, *Treatise*, pp. 378ff.

4. Spooner, *Parson and People*, pp. 54-55.

5. G, 17 December 1856; QR, CXI (April 1862): 403.

6. Evans, *Bishopric of Souls*, pp. 233-37; Gatty, *Vicar and his Duties*, pp. 84-86. Also see G, 10 December 1856.

7. Blunt, *Directorium Pastorale*, p. 290.

8. *Clerical Papers*, p. 9. Also see CO (December 1861), pp. 905-8; Earnshaw, *Church and the Artisan*, p. 9.

9. Kitson Clark, *Churchmen*, pp. 62, 161; Brian Heeney, "Tractarian Pastor: Edward Monro of Harrow Weald. The Pastor's Gifts and Duties," *Canadian Journal of Theology* XIV (1968):24; A. Tindal Hart, *The Curate's Lot* (London, 1970), p. 167; Mackarness and Seymour, *Eighteen Years*, p. 82; CCR (1866), p. 45.

10. Samuel Best, *Parochial Ministrations* (London, 1839), pp. 42-43; Pycroft, *Twenty Years*, p. 188; CCC Minute Book, 30 December 1856; CCR (1864), pp. 191ff. (speech of J. Erskine Clarke). See also Mackenzie, *Ordination Lectures*, p. 199; *PP*, 1857-58, vol. IX, *Spiritual Instruction and Places of Worship*, p. 98 (T. F. Stooks), 188ff. (A. Brady).

11. Ephesians 2:17 and 19; Galatians 3:28.

12. "The Form and Manner of Ordering of Priests," *The Book of Common Prayer*.

13. Wilberforce, *Addresses*, p. 241; Blunt, *Directorium Pastorale*, p. 316; J. L. Brereton, *The Failures of Our Ministry: Their Cause and Remedy* (Barnstaple, 1857), p. 4; Mackenzie, *Ordination Lectures*, p. 81.

14. Brereton, *Failures of Our Ministry*, p. 5.

15. On Girdlestone, see Kitson Clark, *Churchmen*, pp. 178ff.

16. Wilberforce, *Addresses*, p. 242. See also R. A. Soloway, *Prelates and People* (London, 1969), pp. 273ff.

17. Brian Harrison, "Religion and Recreation in Nineteenth-Century England," *Past and Present* XXXVIII (December 1967):121.

18. Edward Monro, *Home and Colonial Missions* (London, 1857), p. 24. See Sandford, *Mission and Extension*, p. 67; Earnshaw, *Church and the Artisan*, p. 6.

19. On separate class services, see above chapter III, p. 36, and Cadman in CCR (1863), p. 179; for voluntary class segregation in church, see Molyneux in *PP*, 1857-58, vol. IX, *Spiritual Instruction and Places of Worship*, pp. 322-23; on separate forms of family prayer, see OCA Minute Book 6, 4 June 1855; on the development of monochrome class neighborhoods in Liverpool, see evidence of Abraham Hume in *PP*, 1857-58, vol. IX, *Spiritual Instruction and Places of Worship*, pp. 453, 455, 461.

20. Jones, *Priest and Parish*, pp. 55-56. For similar views, see Samuel Best, *A Manual of Parochial Institutions with Rules and Regulations and Remarks Explanatory of Their Objects*, 2d ed. (London, 1849), p. 24; Frances E. Kingsley, ed., *Charles Kingsley: His Letters and Memories of His Life* (London, 1890), p. 208; speech by T. J. Rowsell in CCR (1863), pp. 95ff.; Lyttelton's speech in CCR (1866), p. 46.

21. Best, *Parochial Ministrations*, pp. 44-45; Jones, *Priest and Parish*, p. 57. Also see William H. Lyttelton, *A Clergyman's Address to His Parishioners on Church Services, Almsgiving and Other Subjects* (London,

1852), pp. 19ff.; Pycroft, *Twenty Years,* p. 158; Mackenzie, *Ordination Lectures,* p. 116.

22. Champneys, *Parish Work,* p. 28; Lyttelton, *A Clergyman's Address,* pp. 20-24; Gregory, *Difficulties,* pp. 41-43. Also see Spooner, *Parson and People,* p. 58; Jones, *Priest and Parish,* pp. 59-66; Owen Chadwick, *Victorian Miniature* (London, 1960), p. 54; Robert Liddell, *A Pastoral Letter to the Parishioners of St. Paul's, Knightsbridge and St. Barnabas, Pimlico* (London, 1853), p. 14.

23. Jones, *Dead Leaves,* p. 102.

24. Some self-help schemes supported by clergy and gentry actually involved a good deal of paternalism and patronage, and can be called "self-help" only in a modified sense. See Peter H. J. H. Gosden, *Self-Help: Voluntary Associations in Nineteenth-Century Britain* (London, 1973), pp. 33, 65.

25. Best, *A Manual,* pp. 25, 35; Liddell, *Pastoral Letter,* pp. 19-20; Gregory, *Difficulties,* pp. 39-40; Sandford, *Parochialia,* p. 356. For a good discussion of allotments, see Kitson Clark, *Churchmen,* pp. 168ff.

26. J. Erskine Clarke, *Penny Banks* (London, 1859), pp. 12-14.

27. Ridley, *Parochial Duties,* p. 29; *PP,* 1857-58, vol. IX, *Spiritual Instruction and Places of Worship,* p. 68. Also see Gosden, *Self-Help,* pp. 210-12.

28. Blunt, *Directorium Pastorale,* pp. 339-47; Clarke, *Penny Banks.* Also see Mackenzie, *Ordination Lectures,* p. 113.

29. Best, *A Manual,* pp. 27-28 (on Best, see Gosden, *Self-Help,* pp. 105-6); Sandford, *Parochialia,* pp. 351-53. For other examples of such funds, see Liddell, *Pastoral Letter,* p. 16; Spooner, *Parson and People,* pp. 64-65.

30. OCA Minute Book 10, 5 December 1859. See Gosden, *Self-Help,* pp. 22-24.

31. *Parish and the Priest,* pp. 263-72.

32. QR, CII (1857):456ff.

33. Phillip Elliott, *The Sociology of the Professions* (London, 1972), pp. 32ff. See the pamphlet by "a Physician" entitled *Instructions for the Relief of the Sick Poor in Some Diseases of Frequent Occurrence, Addressed to a Parochial Clergyman Residing at a Distance from Professional Aid,* 2d ed. (Gloucester, 1820).

34. Ridley, *Parochial Duties,* pp. 37-38. Also see Pycroft, *Twenty Years,* p. 148; Chadwick, *Victorian Miniature,* pp. 53, 55; Alan Bell, *Sydney Smith, Rector of Foston, 1806-29* (York, 1972), pp. 13-14. For the change by the sixties, see Mackenzie, *Ordination Lectures,* pp. 116-17; Jones, *Priest and Parish,* pp. 48-49.

35. See OCA Minute Book 9, 8 March 1858; Sandford, *Parochialia,* pp. 382ff.; Jones, *Dead Leaves,* pp. 92-93.

36. Sandford, *Parochialia,* pp. 342ff.; Liddell, *Pastoral Letter,* pp. 13-14; and George Nugee, *A Sermon on Church Dispensaries* (London, 1852), pp. 11ff.; *Parish and the Priest,* pp. 240ff. Dispensaries of one sort or another were found in many parishes during this period. See Spooner,

Parson and People, p. 65; Stephens, *Hook*, p. 125; Kitson Clark, *Churchmen*, pp. 202-4. For the organization of similar services by friendly societies, see Gosden, *Self-Help*, pp. 112-13.

37. *PP*, 1857-58, vol. IX, *Spiritual Instruction and Places of Worship*, p. 149; Jones, *Dead Leaves*, pp. 24-26. See also the work of a remarkable layman, Antonio Brady, in *PP*, 1857-58, vol. IX, *Spiritual Instruction and Places of Worship*, pp. 188ff.; and Blunt, *Directorium Pastorale*, pp. 397-98. On the work of the clergy in public health, see Kitson Clark, *Churchmen*, pp. 196ff.

38. J. Erskine Clarke, *Recreations of the People, Real and Imaginary* (London, 1858), p. 7; Huntington, *Amusements*, p. 25; Lyttelton's speech in CCR (1866), p. 49.

39. See Brian Harrison, "Religion and Recreation," pp. 121-22.

40. Blunt, *Directorium Pastorale*, pp. 360ff.; Burgon, *Treatise*, pp. 383ff.; speech by J. C. Chambers in CCR (1869), p. 134. Also see Huntington, *Amusements*, pp. 28-29, 74ff.

41. R. W. Malcolmson, *Popular Recreations in English Society, 1700-1850* (Cambridge, 1973), p. 151.

42. Huntington, *Amusements*, p. 45; Clarke, *Recreations*, pp. 9, 16ff.; Clarke in CCR (1869), p. 123.

43. Burgon, *Treatise*, p. 387. See also Mackarness and Seymour, *Eighteen Years*, pp. 108-10; Huntington, *Amusements*, p. 50; see the entire discussion on "Recreations of the People" in CCR (1869).

44. Huntington, *Amusements*, p. 38; Clarke, *Recreations*, p. 29.

45. J. Erskine Clarke, *Labourers' Clubs and Working Men's Refreshment Rooms* (London, 1859), p. 7. See above, chapter III, p. 45.

46. John F. C. Harrison, *Learning and Living, 1790-1860: A Study in the History of the English Adult Education Movement* (Toronto, 1961), pp. 177-80.

47. Robert Gregory, *Autobiography* (London, 1912), pp. 68-69. See Clarke, *Labourers' Clubs*, pp. 8ff.

48. Clarke, *Labourers' Clubs*, pp. 16-17, 24-25. On the Dover club, see letter from Henry White in G, 9 February 1859. See also Blunt, *Directorium Pastorale*, pp. 348ff.; Harrison, *Learning and Living*, pp. 180ff.

49. G, 24 January 1855; G, 16 November 1864; Burgon, *Treatise*, p. 388; Ridley, *Parochial Duties*, pp. 14-15; Sandford, *Parochialia*, p. 368; Mackenzie, *Ordination Lectures*, p. 117.

50. *Parish and the Priest*, p. 154; speech by Erskine Clarke in CCR (1868), p. 354.

51. G, 26 October and 9 November 1859, 20 June and 21 November 1860, 26 June 1861, 9 July 1862, 22 June 1864.

52. G, 21 November 1860.

53. CCR (1868), p. 361.

54. Burgon, *Treatise*, pp. 274-75; Champneys, *Parish Work*, pp. 130-34.

55. Blunt, *Directorium Pastorale*, pp. 298-300; Ridley, *Parochial Duties*, p. 26; G, 7 September, 28 September, and 30 November 1859; Gregory, *Account*, p. 10; Gregory, *Difficulties*, pp. 43-44; Bridges, *Christian Minis-*

try, p. 420; CO (January 1852), p. 12; How, "Private Life," p. 221. See the description of such schools in the diocese of York in Harrison, *Learning and Living*, pp. 190-93.

56. Oxenden, *Pastoral Office*, pp. 198-99; G, 7 September 1859; Henry J. Burgess, *Enterprise in Education* (London, 1958), p. 210.

57. Ridley, *Parochial Duties*, p. 27; Liddell, *Pastoral Letter*, p. 10.

58. Champneys, *Parish Work*, pp. 87-93.

59. Ridley, *Parochial Duties*, pp. 21-23; Stephens, *Hook*, p. 124; Bridges, *Christian Ministry*, pp. 397-406; Oxenden, *Pastoral Office*, pp. 196-97; Mackenzie, *Ordination Lectures*, pp. 82-89; Blunt, *Directorium Pastorale*, p. 302; CCR (1868), p. 164. On the growth of Sunday Schools, see Chadwick, *Victorian Church* II:256-57.

60. Jones, *Priest and Parish*, p. 191; for T. J. Rowsell's views, see *PP*, 1857-58, vol. IX, *Spiritual Instruction and Places of Worship*, p. 77; J. Erskine Clarke, *The Children of the People* (London, 1860), pp. 22-23.

61. Blunt, *Directorium Pastorale*, pp. 295-96; *Parish and the Priest*, p. 117; Clarke, *Children*, pp. 6ff.; CO (September 1858), pp. 679-81; Sandford, *Parochialia*, pp. 198-200.

62. See Kitson Clark, *Churchmen*, p. 122; Charles K. F. Brown, *The Church's Part in Education, 1833-1941* (London, 1942), p. 172. Also see Burgess, *Enterprise in Education*, especially chapter 14. For Oxfordshire, see McClatchey, *Oxfordshire Clergy*, p. 154.

63. John Pearson, *The Duty of a Layman in the Church of England: A Paper Read at a Meeting of the Clerical and Lay Union* (London, 1856), pp. 16-17. For other objections to clerical begging, see Evans, *Bishopric of Souls*, p. 176; Pycroft, *Twenty Years*, pp. 226ff.; Blunt, *Directorium Pastorale*, pp. 313-15; Jones, *Priest and Parish*, pp. 219-21. For evidence of clerical begging, see *PP*, 1857-58, vol. IX, *Spiritual Instruction and Places of Worship*, pp. 37 (Colbourne), 77 (Rowsell), 160 (Cadman), 165 (King), 181 (Bazely), 330 (Yorke).

64. Stephens, *Hook*, pp. 284, 289; *PP*, 1857-58, vol. IX, *Spiritual Instruction and Places of Worship*, pp. 105 (Ackworth), 191-95 (Brady). On middle class lay support, see ibid., pp. 191 (Brady), 446 (Rushton).

65. Abraham Hume, *The State and Prospects of the Church in Liverpool* (Liverpool, 1869), p. 33; Jones, *Dead Leaves*, pp. 50-51.

66. Burgess, *Enterprise in Education*, p. 148.

67. Monro, *Parochial Work*, p. 116; Blunt, *Acquirements*, p. 199; Blunt, *Directorium Pastorale*, p. 276; Jones, *Priest and Parish*, pp. 180ff.

68. Monro, *Parochial Work*, pp. 224ff.; Sandford, *Mission and Extension*, p. 152. Also see Blunt, *Acquirements*, p. 186.

69. See Richard Johnson, "Educational Policy and Social Control in Early Victorian England," *Past and Present*, IL (November 1970):119; Gillian Sutherland, *Elementary Education in the Nineteenth Century* (London, 1971), p. 21.

70. Sandford, *Parochialia*, p. 114; Best, *A Manual*, p. 13; Blunt, *Acquirements*, p. 181; Jones, *Priest and Parish*, p. 177; Blunt, *Directorium Pastorale*, p. 273.

71. Blunt, *Acquirements,* p. 183.

72. Best, *A Manual,* p. 16; Lyttelton's speech in CCR (1866), pp. 51-52. See also *Parish and the Priest,* p. 132; R. P. Flindall, "The Parish Priest in Victorian England," *Church Quarterly Review,* CLXVIII (1967): 299.

73. Kitson Clark, *Churchmen,* p. 101; J. M. Goldstrom, *The Social Content of Education, 1808-1870* (Shannon, 1972), p. 177.

74. Best, *Parochial Ministrations,* p. 113; Cecil Wray, *Hughes,* p. 118. Also see *Parish and the Priest,* p. 132; Jones, *Priest and Parish,* p. 175; CCR (1869), p. 394 (Ellerton).

75. Blunt, *Acquirements,* p. 178; Oxenden, *Pastoral Office,* pp. 192-93; Shelford, *Memorial,* p. 45.

76. Burgon, *Treatise,* p. 248; Mackenzie, *Ordination Lectures,* p. 14; Champneys, *Parish Work,* pp. 21-25.

77. Wilberforce, *Addresses,* p. 12; CO (March 1861), p. 179, for Wilson's views. See also Monro, *Parochial Work,* pp. 261-62.

Notes to Chapter V

1. For a modern statement of this tension between divine call and professional competence, see *Theological Colleges for Tomorrow Being the Report of a Working Party Appointed by the Archbishops of Canterbury and York to Consider the Problems of the Theological Colleges of the Church of England* (London, 1968), p. 1.

2. Monro, *Pastoral Life,* pp. 36-37.

3. Monro, *Sermons,* pp. 5ff.; Bridges, *Christian Ministry,* p. 96; Oxenden, *Pastoral Office,* p. 22; Wilberforce, *Addresses,* pp. 7-8, 26-28.

4. Thomson, *Choice of a Profession,* pp. 70, 90, 74. See above, chapter II, p. 28. Thomson considered only *average* clerical incomes, and not extremes of poverty or affluence.

5. Bartrum, *Promotion by Merit,* p. 22; Conybeare, "Ecclesiastical Economy," pp. 106-7.

6. Bullock, *History of Training,* pp. 9-10; Burgon, *Treatise,* pp. x-xi.

7. See above, chapter I, p. 5.

8. See above, chapter II, pp. 30ff.

9. CCR (1867), pp. 297-98 (speech by Sir John Pearson); G, 25 April 1866 (letter from "Habitans in Stagno"). Also see Mackarness and Seymour, *Eighteen Years,* p. 173; CCR (1865), pp. 217-18.

10. Jones, *Priest and Parish,* pp. 49, 216. See also Sandford, *Mission and Extension,* p. 124; Jones, *Dead Leaves,* p. 74.

11. QR, CII (1857):462-63; Best, *Parochial Ministrations,* pp. 13-14; CC (1863), pp. 1218-20; Burgon, *Treatise,* pp. ixff.; CCR (1865), p. 232; John W. Diggle, *The Lancashire Life of Bishop Fraser* (London, 1889), pp.

222-23; F. W. B. Bullock discusses the relevant debates in convocation and church congresses (*History of Training,* pp. 129ff.). See also numerous articles on the subject in the church press, e. g., G, 28 June 1848, 8 December 1852, 2 December 1863; CO (February 1854), pp. 79ff.; CRem, XIII (April 1847): 277ff.; CRem XLIII (1862): 70-71.

12. Mackarness and Seymour, *Eighteen Years,* p. 171.

13. CCR (1864), pp. 201-3 (Henry Alford); Reichel, "University Reform." See above, chapter II, p. 31.

14. William R. Ward, *Victorian Oxford* (London, 1965), pp. 249ff.; John Frederick Maurice, *Life of Frederick Denison Maurice,* 2 vols. (London, 1884) II:542; Arthur Westcott, *Life and Letters of Brooke Foss Westcott,* 2 vols. (London, 1903), I:375ff.; Bullock, *History of Training.*

15. Oxenden, *Pastoral Office,* p. 17; CO (June 1855), p. 374; CO (July 1865), pp. 556-57.

16. Bullock, *History of Training,* pp. 62-63, 82-84, 107-8.

17. Ashton Oxenden, *The History of My Life: An Autobiography* (London, 1891), p. 38; Oxenden, *Pastoral Office,* pp. 18, 20. Also see Bridges, *Christian Ministry,* pp. 64-65; *PP,* 1857-58, vol. IX, *Spiritual Instruction and Places of Worship,* p. 187; Whately, *Parochial System,* p. 35; Sandford, *Mission and Extension,* p. 137; Champneys, *Parish Work,* pp. 34-35. For book lists, see Blunt, *Acquirements,* chapters II, III, and IV; Burgon, *Treatise,* chapter IV.

18. CC (1863), pp. 1220-21 (Oxenden); CCR (1865), pp. 104-5 (Hook). On comparisons with other professional training (medicine and law), see Oxenden, *Pastoral Office,* p. 20; *Parish and the Priest,* pp. 49-50; Champneys, *Parish Work,* pp. 34-35; CCR (1863), p. 62 (Stowell); Charles J. Vaughan, *Addresses to Young Clergymen* (London, 1875), pp. ix-x.

19. Bullock, *History of Training,* p. 118; Vaughan, *Addresses to Young Clergymen,* p. xii; CCR (1864), p. 221 (Girdlestone); Sandford, *Mission and Extension,* p. 137; G, 15 November 1865 (G. H. Wilkinson).

20. *PP,* 1857-58, vol. IX, *Spiritual Instruction and Places of Worship,* p. 164 (King); Owen Chadwick, *The Founding of Cuddesdon* (Oxford, 1954), p. 23; Meacham, *Lord Bishop,* pp. 201-2; Manning, *Charge;* Freeman, *A Plea,* p. 27; Henry P. Liddon, *Clerical Life and Work* (London, 1894), pp. 46ff. Also see letter from "C. E. P." in G, 9 November 1864.

21. Liddon, *Clerical Life,* pp. 1, 50, 57; Freeman, *A Plea,* p. 39.

22. Manning, *Charge,* p. 43; Freeman, *A Plea,* pp. 23-27; CCR (1866), p. 112 (Owen); Liddon, *Clerical Life,* pp. 65ff.; G, 8 April 1868 (letter from "Presbyter Anglicanus").

23. Freeman's speech in CC (1865), pp. 2344-45; QR (1857), p. 160; Chadwick, *Cuddesdon,* p. 54. The Evangelical *Christian Observer* advocated colleges for graduates in 1855 (pp. 522-23) and 1857 (pp. 138 and 163).

24. G, 20 May 1863; Ward, *Victorian Oxford,* pp. 123, 138, 263-64.

25. For the development of theological colleges and courses at the new universities, see Bullock, *History of Training;* G, 25 April 1866 (letter from "Habitans in Stagno").

26. Minutes of the Council, St. Aidan's College, 18 March 1867. The

syllabus is found in the college prospectus for 1865, available in the St. Aidan's Archives.

27. *PP*, 1857-58, vol. IX, *Spiritual Instruction and Places of Worship*, pp. 383 and 385 (Baylee). In 1857 the regular or pastoral visitation (i. e., excluding the "statistical") included thirty thousand families (ibid., p. 385; Hume, *Missions at Home*, p. 27). On the formation of the Parochial Assistant Association, see Joseph Baylee, *Report on the Formation and Progress of the Liverpool Parochial Assistant Association and of Birkenhead Theological College* (Birkenhead, 1849); Baylee, *Theological Colleges*, p. 7; Joseph Baylee, *Report to the Committee of St. Aidan's College, Birkenhead* (Birkenhead, 1854), pp. 7-8. For an example of the view that theological and practical training must be kept separate, see *PP*, 1857-58, vol. IX, *Spiritual Instruction and Places of Worship*, p. 308 (G. Nugee).

28. *PP*, 1857-58, vol. IX, *Spiritual Instruction and Places of Worship*, pp. 387-88; Baylee, *Theological Colleges*, p. 5. There was a considerable controversy on the question of Baylee's alleged recruiting activities among Wesleyan ministers. (See Minutes of the Council, 1867-68, and clippings in the St. Aidan's Archives.) According to an article in *The Orb* (28 June 1866), "nearly fifty itinerants and local preachers" attended St. Aidan's in the years 1865-66.

29. G, 23 September, 7 October, 21 October, 4 November, and 11 November 1863. "Parents and Ages of Men" includes a butcher, a printer, a carpenter, and a good many others of similar social rank. For more information on Baylee and his college, see F. B. Heiser, *The Story of St. Aidan's College, Birkenhead* (Chester, 1947).

30. CCR (1869), p. 78 (How). See also Oxenden, *Pastoral Office*, pp. 272-73.

31. CC (1858), p. 88 (Oxenden); Champneys, *Parish Work*, p. 10; CC (1863), p. 1222 (Sandford).

32. CO (March 1861), pp. 177-78 (Wilson); Diggle, *Life of Bishop Fraser*, p. 162 (Fraser); Stephens, *Hook*, pp. 476-77 (Hook); Shelford, *Memorial*, p. 72 (Cadman); *PP*, 1857-58, vol. IX, *Spiritual Instruction and Places of Worship*, pp. 133-34 (Champneys). On the curate's reading, see How, "Private Life," pp. 212-13. For examples of reviews, see CRem, XX (1850):203 (Keble on Monro); CRem, XXXII (1856):510 (J. J. Blunt); CO (December 1856), p. 823 (J. J. Blunt); QR, CII (1857):469 (J. J. Blunt); CRem, XXXV (1858):251 (Oxenden); CO (September 1860), p. 638 (Whately); CRem, XXXIX (1860):454 (Wilberforce); CRem, XLVIII (1864):254 (Burgon); G, 8 February 1865 (J. H. Blunt); CO (May 1866), p. 398 (Champneys).

33. Michael Hennell, *John Venn and the Clapham Sect* (London, 1958), p. 84.

34. On Islington, see *Present Danger and Present Duty: The Papers Read at the Meeting of Clergymen at Islington in January 1868* (London, 1868); also see E. A. Stuart, *Funeral Sermon for the Late Reverend Daniel Wilson, Vicar of Islington and Rural Dean* (London, 1886). Also see CO

(June 1862), pp. 478-79; CR (1868), p. 576; G, 25 August 1858.

35. See Mackarness and Seymour, *Eighteen Years* (for the Alcester meeting), and the unpublished minute books of the Oxford Clerical Association and the Curates' Clerical Club. Also see Burgon, *Treatise*, pp. 394-95; Flindall, "The Parish Priest in Victorian England."

36. CO (January 1861), pp. 28-29; G, 11 May 1864 (leading article on "The Church Institution"). See S. L. Ollard and G. Crosse, eds., *A Dictionary of English Church History* (London, 1912), pp. 527-28.

37. CR, I (1966):254; CO (December 1869), pp. 887ff. Also see Thompson, *Bureaucracy and Church Reform*, pp. 97ff.

38. Ibid., pp. 102ff.; *Present Danger*, p. 130.

39. QR, CXXIII (July 1867): 232-33.

40. On the plight of assistant curates, see *The Whole Case of the Unbeneficed Clergy, or, a Full, Candid, and Impartial Enquiry into the Position of those Clergy Commonly Called the Curates of the Established Church* (London, n. d. [1843]); A Liverpool Curate, *An Appeal to the Incumbents and People of Liverpool* (London, 1857). The *Guardian* frequently published letters on this subject, e. g., 4 February, 26 August, 9 September, and 23 September 1863. Also see Hart, *The Curate's Lot*, chapter 6.

41. Bartrum, *Promotion by Merit*, pp. 5-6. Chadwick, *Victorian Church*, II:207ff. Bartrum's estimate of just under half the benefices of England and Wales in private hands excludes those in the gift of trustees.

42. On 21 February 1855 a correspondent to the *Guardian* wrote that "nepotism and political influence . . . enter largely into the appointment to Chancellor's and Crown Livings," and a leading article in the same journal a dozen years later (9 January 1867) asserts that the same conditions persisted, though in a "less uniformly corrupt" way. The same is asserted of cathedral appointments by the same writers (also see G, 9 September 1863, leading article on "curates"). But Conybeare claimed that, in the fifties, crown appointments were improving (ER, IC [January 1854] :103). On college appointments, see Chadwick, *Victorian Church*, II:208.

43. Bartrum, *Promotion by Merit*, pp. 20-21.

44. *The Whole Case*, pp. 29-31; Best, *Temporal Pillars*, p. 327. On Lonsdale and Wilberforce, see CCR (1867), p. 104; and Meacham, *Lord Bishop*, p. 109. Trollope, *Clergymen*, p. 30. Bartrum, *Promotion by Merit*, p. 17.

45. CCR (1867), p. 103. See also A Liverpool Curate, *An Appeal*, pp. 9-10; Hart, *The Curate's Lot*, pp. 171-73.

46. *The Whole Case*, p. 19; G, 24 November 1858 (letter from "Probitas"); A Liverpool Curate, *An Appeal*, p. 10.

47. Conybeare, "Ecclesiastical Economy," pp. 110-12; QR (January 1858), p. 177; CCR (1863), pp. 70-71.

48. CCR (1863), p. 71 (Espin). Mackarness and Seymour, *Eighteen Years*, p. 90; CCR (1867), p. 99.

49. Bartrum, *Promotion by Merit*, pp. 24-25. Also see G, 21 February

1855 (letter from "M. N."); G, 20 October 1858 (leading article); G, 9 September 1863 (leading article); G, 21 March 1866 (leading article); Trollope, *Clergymen,* pp. 28-30.

50. Bartrum, *Promotion by Merit,* pp. 17ff.

51. Conybeare, "Ecclesiastical Economy," p. 125; Chadwick, *Victorian Church,* II:207.

52. CR, I (January 1866):172. Also see CO (January 1863), p. 48.

53. CCR (1866), p. 132.

54. CR, IV (January 1867):35.

55. Jones, *Priest and Parish,* p. 72; CCR (1869), p. 361 (Abraham Hume).

56. On the extent of private means among the clergy at the end of the century, see Douglas Macleane, "The Church as a Profession," *The National Review* XXXIII (August 1899):952. G, 17 December 1862 (letter from C. A. Fowler).

57. A common proposal was that of a home for worn-out clergymen. See, for example, the correspondence in the *Guardian* on 17 December, 24 December, and 31 December 1862.

58. CC (1857), p. 79.

59. Best, *Temporal Pillars,* pp. 505-6, 511.

BIBLIOGRAPHY

I. MANUSCRIPT SOURCES

Liverpool, England. Church House. Minutes of the Council, 1857-68. St. Aidan's College, Birkenhead.

Liverpool, England. Church House. Parents and Ages of Men Admitted, 1869-71. St. Aidan's College, Birkenhead.

Liverpool, England. Church House. Report of the Finance Committee, 1863. St. Aidan's College, Birkenhead.

London, England. St. Paul's Cathedral Library. Curates' Clerical Club Minute Books.

Oxford, England. The Bodleian Library. Oxford Clerical Association Minute Books, 1851-69.

II. PRINTED WORKS PUBLISHED BEFORE 1900

Arden, G. *The Cure of Souls.* Oxford, 1858.

Arnold, Thomas. *Principles of Church Reform.* 1833. Reprint London, 1962.

Baird, William. *Revival of the Subdiaconate: A Plea for the*

Extension of the Ministerial Office. A Letter to the Rt. Hon. and Rt. Rev. the Lord Bishop of London. London, 1865.

Bartrum, Edward. *Promotion by Merit Essential to the Progress of the Church.* London, 1866.

Baylee, Joseph. *Report of the Formation and Progress of the Liverpool Parochial Assistant Association and of Birkenhead Theological College.* Birkenhead, 1849.

———— *Report to the Committee of St. Aidan's College,* Birkenhead. [Birkenhead, 1854].

———— *Theological Colleges: Their True Use and Their Important Bearing Upon the Theological Education of the Clergy.* London, 1855.

———— *Principal's Report Upon St. Aidan's Theological College, Presented to the Council.* London, 1868.

Bentham, Jeremy. *The Handbook of Political Fallacies.* Harper Torchbook ed. New York, 1962.

Best, Samuel. *Parochial Ministrations.* London, 1839.

———— *A Manual of Parochial Institutions with Rules and Regulations and Remarks Explanatory of their Objects.* 2d ed. London, 1849.

Blunt, John H. *Directorium Pastorale. Principles and Practice of Pastoral Work in the Church of England.* London, 1864.

Blunt, John J. *The Acquirements and Principal Obligations and Duties of the Parish Priest: Being a Course of Lectures Delivered at the University of Cambridge to the Students in Divinity.* London, 1856.

Brereton, J. L. *The Failures of Our Ministry: Their Cause and Remedy.* Barnstaple, 1857.

Bridges, Charles. *The Christian Ministry; with an Inquiry into the Causes of its Inefficiency: with an Especial Reference to the Ministry of the Establishment.* 6th ed. London, 1844.

Burgon, John W. *A Treatise on the Pastoral Office, Addressed Chiefly to Candidates for Holy Orders or to Those Who Have Recently Undertaken the Cure of Souls.* London, 1864.

Carus, William. *The Christian Ministry. An Address Delivered to the Clergy of Plymouth Combined Clerical Meeting, June 28, 1865.* Cambridge, 1866.

Champneys, William Weldon. *Parish Work: A Brief Manual for the Younger Clergy.* London, 1866.

Cheering Words for the Christian Wayfarer. London, 1859.

Christian Observer.

Christian Remembrancer.

Chronicle of Convocation.

Church Congress Reports.

Clarke, J. Erskine. *Recreations of the People, Real and Imaginary.* London, 1858.

——— *Penny Banks.* London, 1859.

——— *Labourers' Clubs and Working Men's Refreshment Rooms.* London, 1859.

——— *The Children of the People.* London, 1860.

——— *Cheap Books and How to Use Them.* Oxford, 1861.

Clergymen and Doctors. Edinburgh, n. d.

Clerical Papers by One of Our Club. London, 1861.

Clerical Recreations: Thoughts for the Clergy by One of Themselves. London, 1863.

Contemporary Review

Country Curate. *The Clergyman's Private Register and Assistant in His Ministerial Visits.* London, 1838.

Crockford's Clerical Directory.

Davidson, Randall T., and Benham, William. *Life of Archibald Campbell Tait.* 2 vols. London, 1891.

Davies, John. *The Subdivision and Re-Arrangement of Parishes.* London, 1849.

The Deficient Supply of Well-Qualified Clergymen for the Church of England at the Present Time. Birkenhead, 1863.

Diggle, John W. *The Lancashire Life of Bishop Fraser.* London, 1889.

Earnshaw, S. *The Church and the Artisan: A Sermon Preached on Sunday Morning, February 10, 1861, in the Parish Church, Sheffield.* London, 1861.

Edinburgh Review.

Espin, Thomas E. *Our Want of Clergy, Its Causes and Suggestions for Its Cure: A Sermon Preached before the University of Oxford.* London, 1863.

Evans, R. W. *The Bishopric of Souls.* London, 1842.

Freeman, Philip. *A Plea for the Education of the Clergy.* London, 1851.

Gatty, Alfred. *The Vicar and His Duties.* London, 1853.

Good Words.

Great Britain, *Parliamentary Papers,* 1857-58, vol. IX. *Report from the Select Committee of the House of Lords Appointed to Inquire into the Deficiency of Means of Spiritual Instruction and Places of Worship in the Metropolis and Other Populous Places in England and Wales, Especially in the Mining and Manufacturing Districts.*

Gregory, Robert. *What is the Spiritual Condition of the Metropolis? And Who is Responsible? A Sermon Preached before the University at St. Mary's Church in Oxford.* Oxford, 1860.

_____ *How is Clerical Destitution to be Prevented?* London, 1860.

_____ *Account of the Schools and Charities in Connexion with the District Church of St. Mary-the-Less Lambeth.* London, 1863.

_____ *The Difficulties and the Organisation of a Poor Metropolitan Parish. Two Lectures Delivered on the 16th and 17th November 1865 to the Students at the Theological College Cuddesdon.* London, 1866.

Guardian.

Hale, W. H. *The Duties of Deacons and Priests in the Church of England Compared: With Suggestions for the Extension of the Order of Deacons and the Establishment of an Order of Sub-Deacons.* London, 1850.

_____ *Suggestions for the Extension of the Ministry and the Revival of the Order of Sub-Deacons: A Charge Delivered to the Clergy of the Archdeaconry of London, May 24, 1852.* London, 1852.

Heanley, R. M. *A Memoir of Edward Steere, DD, LLD, Third Missionary Bishop of Central Africa.* London, 1888.

[Hessey, Francis]. *Hints to District Visitors.* London, 1858.

Heygate, W. E. *Ember Hours.* London, 1857.

Hints to Young Clergymen. London, n. d. [1874].

How, W. Walsham. *Pastor in Parochia.* London, n. d. [1868].

_____ *Lectures on Parochial Work Delivered in the Divinity School Cambridge, 1883.* 2d ed. London, 1884.

Hume, Abraham. *Missions at Home, or a Clergyman's Account of a Portion of the Town of Liverpool.* London, 1850.

_____ *Suggestions for the Advancement of Literature and Learning in Liverpool.* Liverpool, 1851.

_____ *Conditions of Liverpool, Religious and Social; Including Notices of the State of Education and Morals, Pauperism and Crime.* 2d ed. Liverpool, 1858.

_____ *The Church of England the Home Missionary to the Poor,*

Especially in Our Large Towns. Written in Reply to the Articles of Herbert S. Skeats, Esq., in the "Nonconformist" Newspaper on "Dissent in Poor Populous Districts." London, 1862.

—— *The State and Prospects of the Church in Liverpool.* Liverpool, 1869.

Huntington, George. *Amusements and the Need of Supplying Healthy Recreations for the Poor.* 2d ed. Oxford, 1868.

Ince, William. *Holy Orders: The Call and the Preparation. Two Sermons Preached in Exeter College Chapel in Michaelmas Term, 1862.* Oxford, 1862.

Jackson, John. *Rest Before Labour. The Advantages and Disadvantages of Theological Colleges.* London, 1859.

Jervis, W. G. *The Poor Condition of the Clergy and the Causes Considered with Suggestions for Remedying the Same.* London, 1856.

Jones, Harry. *Some Grateful Thoughts and Some Grave Anxieties About a London District.* London, 1853.

—— *Priest and Parish.* London, 1866.

—— *East and West London.* London, 1875.

—— *Fifty Years or Dead Leaves and Living Seeds.* London, 1895.

Kendall, James. *Rambles of an Evangelist.* London, 1853.

Liddell, Robert. *A Pastoral Letter to the Parishioners of St. Paul's, Knightsbridge and St. Barnabas, Pimlico.* London, 1853.

Liddon, Henry P. *Clerical Life and Work.* London, 1894.

A Liverpool Curate. *An Appeal to the Incumbents and People of Liverpool.* London, 1857.

Liverpool Mercury.

Lloyd, Henry Robert. *The Responsibilities and Requirements of the Clergy.* Durham, 1857.

Lowder, C. L. *Twenty-one Years at St. George's Mission.* London, 1877.

Lyttelton, William H. *A Clergyman's Address to his Parishioners on Church Services, Almsgiving, and Other Subjects.* London, 1852.

—— *Following the Leadings of God in Nature and in Providence. The Duty of Christ's Ministers. An Ordination Sermon.* London, 1871.

Mackarness, J. F., and Seymour, R., eds. *Eighteen Years of a Clerical Meeting.* London, 1862.

Mackenzie, Henry. *On the Parochial System as a Means of Al-*

leviating Temporal Distress in the Metropolis. London, 1850.

———— *Service, not Rule, the Work of the Ministry. An Ordination Sermon Preached on the Fourth Sunday in Advent in the Cathedral of Lincoln.* London, 1856.

———— *The Parochial System: Its Development and Results. A Sermon.* London, 1858.

———— *Ordination Lectures, delivered in Riseholme Palace Chapel During Ember Weeks.* London, 1862.

Macmillan's Magazine.

Manning, Henry E. *A Charge Delivered at the Ordinary Visitation of the Archdeaconry of Chichester in July 1846.* London, 1846.

Maurice, John Frederick. *The Life of Frederick Denison Maurice.* 2 vols. London, 1884.

Miall, Edward. *The Nonconformist's Sketch Book.* New ed. London, 1867.

———— *The British Churches in Relation to the British People.* 2d ed. London, 1850.

———— *The Social Influences of the State Church.* London, 1867.

Monro, Edward. *The Fulfilment of the Ministry. A Sermon Preached before Some Clergy of the Diocese of Worcester.* London, 1848.

———— *Sermons Principally on the Responsibilities of the Ministerial Office.* Oxford, 1850.

———— *Parochial Work.* London, 1850.

———— *The Parish.* 2d ed. Oxford, 1853.

———— *Home and Colonial Missions: Two Sermons.* London, 1857.

———— *The Navvies and How to Meet Them: A Letter to a Friend.* London, 1857.

———— *Pastoral Life.* London, 1862.

Morley, John Cooper. *A Brief Memoir of the Reverend Abraham Hume.* Liverpool, 1887.

National Review.

Nugee, George. *A Sermon on Church Dispensaries.* London, 1852.

Oxenden, Ashton. *The Pastoral Office: Its Duties, Difficulties, Privileges and Prospects.* London, 1857.

———— *The History of My Life: An Autobiography.* London, 1891.

The Parish and the Priest: Colloquies on the Pastoral Care and Parochial Institutions of a Country Village. London, 1858.

Pearson, John. *The Duty of a Layman in the Church of England: A Paper Read at a Meeting of the Clerical and Lay Union.* London, 1856.

A Physician. *Instructions for the Relief of the Sick Poor in Some Diseases of Frequent Occurence, Addressed to a Parochial Clergyman Residing at a Distance from Professional Aid.* 2d ed. Gloucester, 1820.

Pinnock, W. H. *The Laws and Usages of the Church and Clergy.* Cambridge, 1855-63.

Present Danger and Present Duty: The Papers Read at the Meeting of Clergymen at Islington in January 1868. London, 1868.

Pycroft, James. *Twenty Years in the Church: An Autobiography.* 4th ed. London, 1861.

Quarterly Review.

Report of the Formation and Progress of the Liverpool Parochial Assistant Association and of Birkenhead Theological College. Birkenhead, 1849.

[Ridley, H. C.] *Parochial Duties, Practically Illustrated.* 2d ed. Henley-on-Thames, 1829.

Rigg, J. H. *The Relations of John Wesley and of Wesleyan Methodism to the Church of England.* London, 1868.

Sandford, John. *Parochialia, or Church, School and Parish.* London, 1845.

_____. *The Mission and Extension of the Church at Home. Bampton Lectures, 1861.* London, 1862.

Shelford, Leonard E. *A Memorial of the Reverend William Cadman, M.A.* London, 1899.

Spooner, Edward, *Parson and People, or Incidents in the Everyday Life of a Clergyman.* 2d ed. London, 1864.

Stephens, William R. W. *The Life and Letters of Walter Farquhar Hook.* 7th ed. London, 1885.

Stephenson, Nash. *On the Rise and Progress of the Movement for the Abolition of Statutes, Mops, or Feeing Markets.* London, 1861.

Stoughton, John. *Religion in England from 1800 to 1850.* 2 vols. London, 1884.

Stuart, E. A. *Funeral Sermon for the Late Reverend Daniel Wilson, Vicar of Islington and Rural Dean.* London, 1886.

Sumner, Charles Richard. *A Charge Delivered to the Clergy of the Diocese of Winchester.* London, 1862.

Sweet, J. B. *Speculum Parochiale, According to a Form Prepared by J. B. Sweet.* London, 1859.

[Talbot, C. S.] *A Servant of the Poor, or Some Account of the Life and Death of a Parochial Mission Woman.* London, 1874.

"Tekel." *The Views of a Church of England Layman Relative to the Church of England Clergy With Some Suggestions on the Subject of Lay Agency*. London, 1866.

Thompson, Henry. *Pastoralia: A Manual of Helps for the Parochial Clergy*. London, 1830.

Thomson, H. B. *The Choice of a Profession*. London, 1857.

The Times.

Trollope, Anthony. *Clergymen of the Church of England*. London, 1866.

Vaughan, Charles J. *Addresses to Young Clergymen*. London, 1875.

Voysey, Charles. *The Liberal Clergy*. Ramsgate, 1868.

Weir, A., and Maclagan, W. D., eds. *The Church and the Age: Essays on the Principles and Present Position of the Anglican Church*. London, 1870.

Whately, Richard. *Letter to a Clergyman*. Dublin, 1836.

———. *The Parochial System: Being the Charge Delivered at the Triennial Visitation of the Province of Dublin*. Dublin, 1859.

———. *The Parish Pastor*. London, 1860.

The Whole Case of the Unbeneficed Clergy, or, a Full, Candid, and Impartial Enquiry into the Position of those Clergy Commonly Called the Curates of the Established Church. London, n. d. [1843].

Wilberforce, Henry W. *The Parochial System: An Appeal to English Churchmen*. London, 1838.

Wilberforce, Samuel. *The Notebook of a Country Clergyman*. London, 1833.

———. *Addresses to the Candidates for Ordination on the Questions of the Ordination Service*. 2d ed. London, 1860.

Wray, Cecil. *Four Years of Pastoral Work, Being a Sketch of the Ministerial Labours of the Rev. Edward John Rees Hughes*. London, 1854.

III. Printed Works Published After 1900

Anderson, Olive. "The Growth of Christian Militarism in Mid-Victorian Britain." *English Historical Review* LXXXVI (January 1971):46-72.

Bell, Alan. *Sydney Smith, Rector of Foston, 1806-29*. York, 1972.

Best, Geoffrey F. A. *Temporal Pillars: Queen Anne's Bounty, the Ecclesiastical Commissioners and the Church of England.* Cambridge, 1964.

Brown, Charles K. F. *The Church's Part in Education, 1833-1941.* London, 1942.

Bullock, Friederick W. B. *A History of Training for the Ministry of the Church of England in England and Wales from 1800 to 1874.* St. Leonard's-on-Sea, 1955.

Burgess, Henry J. *Enterprise in Education.* London, 1958.

Chadwick, Owen. *The Founding of Cuddesdon.* Oxford, 1954.

───── *Victorian Miniature.* London, 1960.

───── *The Victorian Church.* 2 vols. London, 1966 and 1970.

Deacon, Alan, and Hill, Michael. "The Problem of Surplus Women in the Nineteenth Century: Secular and Religious Alternatives." *A Sociological Yearbook of Religion in Britain.* London, 1972.

Dunbabin, John P. D. *Rural Discontent in Nineteenth-Century Britain.* London, 1974.

Elliott, Philip. *The Sociology of the Professions.* London, 1972.

Evans, Eric J. "Some Reasons for the Growth of English Rural Anticlericalism, c. 1750—c. 1830." *Past and Present* LXVI (February 1975):84-109.

Facts and Figures About the Church of England. London, 1962.

Faulkner, Harold U. *Chartism and the Churches.* New York, 1916.

Firth, Charles Harding. *A Commentary on Macaulay's History of England.* London, 1964.

Flindall, R. P. "The Parish Priest in Victorian England." *Church Quarterly Review* CLXVIII (1967):296-306.

Goldstrom, J. M. *The Social Content of Education, 1808-1870.* Shannon, 1972.

Gosden, Peter H. J. H. *Self-Help: Voluntary Associations in Nineteenth-Century Britain.* London, 1973.

Gregory, Robert. *Autobiography.* London, 1912.

Harrison, Brian. "Religion and Recreation in Nineteenth-Century England." *Past and Present* XXXVIII (December 1967): 98-125.

Harrison, John F. C. *Learning and Living, 1790-1860: A Study in the History of the English Adult Education Movement.* Toronto, 1961.

Hart, A. Tindal. *Clergy and Society, 1600-1800.* London, 1968.

_____ *The Curate's Lot.* London, 1971.

Heeney, Brian. "Tractarian Pastor: Edward Monro of Harrow Weald. The Pastor's Gifts and Duties." *Canadian Journal of Theology* XIII, no. 4 (1967): 242-51 and XIV, no. 1 (1968):13-27.

Heiser, F. B. *The Story of St. Aidan's College, Birkenhead.* Chester, 1947.

Hennell, Michael. *John Venn and the Clapham Sect.* London, 1958.

Hobsbawm, Eric J., and Rudé, George. *Captain Swing.* Penguin ed. London, 1973.

Humphreys, A. R. *The Augustan World.* 2d ed. London, 1964.

Inglis, Kenneth S. *Churches and the Working Classes in Victorian England.* London, 1963.

Johnson, Richard. "Educational Policy and Social Control in Early Victorian England." *Past and Present* IL (November 1970): 96-119.

Kingsley, Frances E., ed. *Charles Kingsley: His Letters and Memories of His Life.* London, 1890.

Kitson Clark, George S. R. *Churchmen and the Condition of England.* London, 1973.

McClatchey, Diana. *Oxfordshire Clergy 1777-1869.* Oxford, 1960.

Macleane, Douglas. "The Church as a Profession." *The National Review* XXXIII (August 1899): 945-55.

Malcolmson, R. W. *Popular Recreations in English Society, 1700-1850.* Cambridge, 1973.

Meacham, Standish. *Lord Bishop: The Life of Samuel Wilberforce, 1805-1873.* Cambridge, Mass., 1970.

Mitchell, Brian R., and Deane, Phyllis. *Abstract of British Historical Statistics.* Cambridge, 1962.

Ollard, S. L., and Crosse, G., eds. *A Dictionary of English Church History.* London, 1912.

Soloway, R. A. *Prelates and People.* London, 1969.

Sykes, Norman. *Church and State in England in the Eighteenth Century.* Cambridge, 1934.

Theological Colleges for Tomorrow Being the Report of a Working Party Appointed by the Archbishops of Canterbury and York to Consider the Problems of the Theological Colleges of the Church of England. London, 1968.

Thompson, Kenneth A. *Bureaucracy and Church Reform.* Oxford, 1970.

Warne, Arthur. *Church and Society in Eighteenth Century Devon.* Newton Abbot, 1969.

Ward, William R. *Victorian Oxford.* London, 1965.

_____ *Religion and Society in England 1790-1850.* London, 1972.

Westcott, Arthur. *Life and Letters of Brooke Foss Westcott.* 2 vols. London, 1903.

Whitehead, Benjamin. *Church Law.* 3d ed. London, 1911.

Zangerl, Carl H. E. "The Social Composition of the County Magistracy in England and Wales, 1831-1887." *Journal of British Studies* XI (November 1971):113-25.

IV. Theses

Coxon, Anthony P. M. "A Sociological Study of the Social Recruitment, Selection, and Professional Socialization of Anglican Ordinands." Ph. D. thesis, University of Leeds, 1965.

Elliott, Charles M. "The Social and Economic History of the Principal Protestant Denominations in Leeds, 1760-1844." D. Phil. thesis, Oxford University, 1962.

Gilbert, A. D. "The Growth and Decline of Nonconformity in England and Wales with Special Reference to the Period Before 1850: An Historical Interpretation of Statistics of Religious Practice." D. Phil. thesis, Oxford University, 1973.

Roberts, M. J. D. "The Role of the Laity in the Church of England, c. 1850-1885." D. Phil. thesis, Oxford University, 1974.

Russell, Anthony John. "A Sociological Analysis of the Clergyman's Role with Special Reference to its Development in the Early Nineteenth Century." D. Phil. thesis, Oxford University, 1970.

INDEX

Morning prayer, 36, 39-40
Mothers' meetings, 86
Music, 80

National Society for Promoting the Education of the Poor in the Principles of the Established Church, 87, 89
Needlewomen, 73
New Testament, 68-69, 76
Newcastle, 27
Nonconformist, the, 128n
Nonconformists, 3-4; *see also* Dissenters
North London Deaconess Institution, 59
Nurseries, 86-87
Nursing care, 77

Occupational guide books, 94
Open air meetings, 37-38
Ordinands, 7, 9, 27-31, 33, 41, 98-102, 106, 118, 126, 133n
Ordination, 7, 11, 15-16, 27, 29-30, 32-34, 41, 94, 98-100, 102, 107, 126
Oxenden, Ashton, bishop of Montreal, 1, 11-13, 15, 20-21, 40, 43, 48, 53-54, 100, 107, 111, 124
Oxford Clerical Association, 75, 109-10
Oxford Movement, 5, 8, 39, 51, 97
Oxford university, 28, 41, 96, 98-102, 107, 126

Parents, 44, 72
Parish organization, 56-58
Parliament, 7, 56, 110, 116-17
Parochial Assistant Association, 105, 147n
Parochial church women, 60
Parochial mission women, 60
Patronage, 7, 28, 55, 111-15
Pearson, John, 96
Peel, Sir Robert, 56
Penny banks, 74-75
Penny gaffes, 80
Pensions, clergy, 116
Personal qualities of clergy, 11-22, 54-55, 93-94, 114

Physicians, 42, 49, 53; *see also* doctors *and* medicine
Plaistow, Essex, 88
Pluckley, Kent, 11
Plumstead, Kent, 88
Police, 76; clergy as preventive police, 66-67
Police, District Inspector of, 52
Poor, the, 2-3, 31, 43-44, 52-53, 57, 67-72, 74, 77, 79, 81; rural, 25, 80; schools for, 90-92; services for, 36-40; urban, 24-27, 30, 36, 60-63, 68; *see also* working classes, workingmen, *and* social classes
Poor Law, 52, 67, 77, 140n
Population, 55, 132n
Poverty, 71-73; *see also* the poor
Poverty of clergy, 23, 28-29, 94, 111-13, 116
Prayer Book, the, 36, 39, 46, 50-51, 63, 95
Preaching, 35-36, 38-44, 60, 97, 114; *see also* sermons
Pregnancy, 72
Professionalization, 77, 118
Promotion, clerical, 7, 19, 94-95, 111-17
Provident societies, 72, 75
Public health, 77-78
Public parks, 81
Pubs, 75-76, 80-83
Pusey, Edward Bouverie, 98-99
Pycroft, James, 16, 18, 20, 32, 68, 124

Queen's College, Birmingham, 104

Radcliffe Infirmary, 109
Radicals, working-class, 3
Railway excursions, 81
Railway navvies, 18
Ratio of clergymen to laymen, 27-28, 133n
Reading, Berkshire, 37
Reading rooms, 83
Reconciliation, 62, 66, 68-70, 80
Recreation for workingmen, 79-84
Reformation, 42, 110
Reichel, Charles Parsons, 29, 124

Theological reading, 42-43, 100-01; *see also* training, theological

Theology, voluntary examinations in, 99

Thirty-Nine Articles, the, 51

Thompson, Henry, 51, 125

Thomson, H. Byerly, 94

Thorp, Charles, 27

Tithe, 23-24

Tractarians, 9, 12, 33, 39, 50-51, 134n

Training, pastoral, 6, 8-9, 29, 96-102, 104-07

Training, theological, 6-9, 102-06

Trench, Francis, 37

Trollope, Anthony, 4, 21, 24, 112

Unchastity, 20

Universities, 23, 28-29, 32, 55, 98-99, 102, 104, 107-08; *see also* under individual institutions

Upper classes, 43, 61, 110; *see also* aristocracy, gentry, social classes *and* squires

Vaccination, 44

Vaughan, Charles John, 101, 125

Vauxhall, Liverpool, 106

Victoria Docks, 88

Villiers, Henry Montagu, bishop of Durham, 110

Visitation of the sick, Prayer Book order for the, 51, 54

Visiting, parochial, 21, 23, 27, 35, 42, 54-55, 63, 106, 109-10, 114; by lay helpers, 60-63; the sick, 9, 51-54, 58, 101

Visiting, social, 13

Vocation, 23, 93-94, 97, 100, 102, 118

Wells theological college, 103

West End of London, the, 62, 109

Westcott, Brooke Foss, bishop of Durham, 99

Whately, Richard, archbishop of Dublin, 48, 125

Whitechapel, London, 32, 60

Wilberforce, Henry William, 55, 125

Wilberforce, Samuel, bishop of Oxford and Winchester, 2, 11-12, 15-16, 20-21, 42-43, 51, 53-55, 69-70, 92, 101, 110-12, 125

Wilson, Daniel, 92, 108-09, 125

Wilson, Thomas, bishop of Sodor and Man, 95

Wiltshire, 30

Working classes, 16, 25-26, 32, 37-38, 61, 68, 70, 74-77, 79, 82-84; *see also* the poor, workingmen, *and* social classes

Workingmen, 8, 25-26, 37, 75, 79, 82, 86; *see also* working classes *and* the poor

Workingmen, wives of, 86

Workingmen's associations, 75, 82; *see also* clubs, parochial

Worldliness of clergy, 20

Worship, 35-39

Worshippers, number of, 40

Wray, Cecil, 14